Sherwood
The Great C...

A Scallywag Bay Story

Jonas Lane

First edition. November 5th 2023

Copyright © 2023 JONAS LANE.

Written by JONAS LANE.

Published by Jonas Lane Writing Ltd.

First published 2023.
©2023 Jonas Lane.

Based on the original short story
'PC Tom and the Great Cake Robbery'
written under the name
'Alan Jones'.
© Jonas Lane. 1999. 2003. 2010. 2023

Inspired by
'The Adventures of Sherlock Holmes'
by Arthur Conan Doyle
First Published in 1862

Publisher's Note: This is a work of fiction. Certain characters and their actions may have been inspired by historical individuals and events as well as characters in the public domain.
The characters in the novel, however, represent the work of the author's imagination. Any resemblance to actual persons, living or dead, is entirely coincidental.

The moral rights of Jonas Lane to be identified as the author of this work has been asserted by him in accordance with the Copyrights, Designs and Patents Act, 1988.

All rights reserved. No part of this publication may be reproduced, stored in a retrieval system, or transmitted in any form or by any means, electronic, mechanical, photocopying, recording or otherwise, without the prior written permission of the author and publisher.

Published in Great Britain.
Cover Design by James, GoOnWrite.com

Sherwood Holmes
The Great Cake Robbery

A Scallywag Bay Story

Jonas Lane

First edition. November 5th 2023

Copyright © 2023 JONAS LANE.

Written by JONAS LANE.

Published by Jonas Lane Writing Ltd.

This is a work of fiction, inspired by literacy characters now in the public domain.
Similarities to people, places or events are entirely coincidental.

Contents

Foreword...page 8
Chapter One...page 10
Chapter Two...page 19
Chapter Three...page 25
Chapter Four...page 32
Chapter Five...page 45
Chapter Six...page 49
Chapter Seven...page 64
Chapter Eight...page 77
Chapter Nine ...page 89
Chapter Ten...page 100
Chapter Eleven...page 112
Chapter Twelve...page 121
Chapter Thirteen...page 136

Sherwood Holmes
The Great Cake Robbery

About the author

Jonas Lane is an acclaimed author and educator who is never happier than when he's telling a tall tale, whether it's to his readers or the children he teaches daily. He has written several books across a number of different genres, including the hugely popular Lord Thyme-Slipp series, regularly fusing historical fact with hysterical fiction

Although predominantly classified as a children's and YA author, Jonas Lane's books appeal to all ages, his reading audience being those that are still young at heart. Every novel Jonas has had published so far has been rated as 5-star by those who have reviewed them, young and old

In addition to writing novels, Jonas Lane is also a published poet and has written articles both locally and nationally, as well as being a former television and music critic for the Bedfordshire Times newspaper.

Jonas lives in a North Bedfordshire village over the hills and faraway…

Visit Jonas at his website
www.jonaslaneauthor.com

For James

Whose brilliant cover designs have given this author and his books a brand new lease of life…

and

For Nick,

For his continued help and support in promoting my writing to a much wider audience.

I thank you both immensely.

JL

Foreword

I am very fortunate in the fact that I get to see the audience I write for on a daily basis working in the amazing primary school that I do.

My local fan base has grown considerably in the past eighteen months ever since I've been encouraged to hold writing assemblies by our fabulous headteacher, Mr Hackett, with children of all ages now becoming more aware of the fact that I am both a writer and a teacher.

All the children love attending these, especially the children in Years 1 and 2 who can't wait to tell me about their own writing, often telling me that they are now writing their own stories or books. That's one of the added joys of being a writer/teacher – inspiring others.

However, it also recently presented me with a delicate but welcome problem with several of the younger children of our school asking me when I would write a book just for them.

"It's half term next week, so you can write it then," was just one of the more helpful suggestions…

Normally, it takes a while to come up with an idea worthy enough of the request made of me, but on this occasion, it was an easy one to fix, taking a short, easy-going but throwaway story I wrote for my then two-year old son to turn it into the book you are reading today, with the odd tweak here and there regarding character names as well as extra stories about the wonderful people who make my beloved Scallywag Bay such a lovely place to revisit and share with you all so many years later.

In addition to this, the main character, originally called PC Tom, was magically transformed into our hero, Sherwood Holmes, a loving homage to the great detective Sherlock Holmes whose books I devoured when I was younger.

As demanded by my youngest fans, I did indeed spend the entire half-term fleshing my story out, adding extra scenes and detail, though it took a little longer for me to complete and polish the final result you hold in your hands today.

So here it is, my dearest and youngest readers, a book with a baker's dozen of chapters, written especially for you, but one I hope will be enjoyed by children – and adults – of all ages.

I hope you enjoy reading this book as much as I've enjoyed writing it for you.

Jonas Lane
November 2023.

Chapter One

It was a bright and sunny day as PC Sherwood Holmes drew back the bedroom window curtains of his new home at 999 Letsby Avenue.

He had only lived there for a couple of months after moving to Scallywag Bay from London where he was once a police detective, just like his great-great-great-great uncle, Sherlock Holmes had been.

But Sherwood didn't think that he was as good a detective nor as clever at catching master criminals as his famous relative had been so asked if he could be transferred far away from the big city to somewhere much quieter, safer and less crime riddled where everyone knew everyone else's name and where people were kinder to one another. That's how he came to be in the sleepy seaside town of Scallywag Bay that fine summer's morning.

Scallywag Bay was a quiet seaside town in the small county of Blinkingshire where nothing strange of unusual ever happened most of the time which suited Sherwood right down to the ground as he had only become a police officer as everyone else in the Holmes family had been in the police force in one way or another now or in the past.

Therefore, it was always expected that Sherwood would follow in their famous footsteps.

Apart from his world-famous great-great-great-great uncle, his great-great-great grandfather Shylock Holmes had also been a police detective at Scotland Yard.

So had his great-great-grandfather, Sherman Holmes…

And his great-grandfather Hemlock Holmes…

And his great grandfather Sherwin Holmes…

As well as his grandfather Shadrick Holmes of course…

Not forgetting his father Shanko Holmes too!

As you can see, Sherwood really had little to no choice but to become a police officer when he grew up which he didn't mind too much as all he really wanted was to help make a difference to people's lives.

However, he never wanted to become as famous as the rest of the Holmes family, nor was he as clever a detective as they, not by a long way, or so he thought…

In fact, all he ever liked or wanted to do was just good old fashioned police work, things that you could never really do when working for New Scotland Yard, like helping someone who might have lost their cat…

Or offering to help someone who might have had their bike stolen and needed a lift to work…

Or by helping a little old woman who might had have difficulty carrying her shopping as she crossed the road…

Or helping a young lady who might need to find their way to the train station one busy morning for a very important appointment….

These things Sherwood wouldn't - or couldn't do – in a big, bustling city like London.

But he could do all of that and much, much more in this sleepy little seaside town where everyone had made him feel so welcome in such the few short months of him moving there.

Yes, Sherwood Holmes really was made for Scallywag Bay and Scallywag Bay really was made for Sherwood Holmes…

The people of Scallywag Bay immediately took to Sherwood almost as soon as he'd arrived in the town. After all, he was a kind, friendly and jolly looking man who didn't seem to have a single bad bone in his body.

No matter what anyone ever said or did to him, Sherwood would always try to see the best in everyone, always giving them a second chance no matter what mistakes they may have made…

Unless it was something very, very serious, of course!

Sherwood smiled to himself as he looked in the mirror that morning, proudly smoothing his smart, dark blue police uniform down, plucking several cat hairs off it, finally happy to be in a place where he truly wanted to be, being a friendly face to everyone who knew him, someone they could call upon and trust whenever they were in danger, in need or in trouble.

Yes, Sherwood Holmes was definitely made for Scallywag Bay and Scallywag Bay definitely was made for Sherwood Holmes…

"Looks like it's going to be a warm one today, Watson," Sherwood shouted across the bedroom towards the basket where Watson, his incredibly large Maine Coon cat who Sherwood had named after Sherlock Holmes' legendary best friend, moaned loudly as he pulled his blanket back over his head.

"Come on, shake a leg!" Sherwood laughed, "I've

got a feeling it's going to be a busy day today."

Watson refused to move so Sherwood slowly went downstairs to put the kettle on.

"I know what will get that lazy old moggy of mine moving this morning," Sherwood said to himself as he went into the fridge and pulled out a pack of jumbo pork sausages.

"Won't be long now…" he smiled to himself as he put the sausages into a frying pan and turned the hob on.

After a few minutes, the sausages began to sizzle and spit as they cooked.

"Delicious," Sherwood said as he took a deep breath and smelt the sausages, "won't be long now…"

As if by magic, there was a loud *thud* upstairs, which was soon followed by the sound of Watson's heavy paws pounding the stairs as the

cat quickly raced down them, two steps as a time.

"Thought that would get you going, lazybones!" Sherwood laughed as he threw a sausage at the old cat who swallowed it down in one huge gulp.

"Where are your manners, Watson?" Sherwood said, putting on his police helmet as Watson wolfed down the rest of the sausages Sherwood had put in his bowl for him.

"Mew, mew," Watson mumbled.

"You're very welcome, my dear Watson!"

After they had both finished their breakfasts, the cat begging and failing to get seconds, Sherwood and Watson went outside his home which had once been a small chapel, the police constable climbed onto his motorcycle as Watson jumped into the sidecar.

"Hold on tight, old boy!" Sherwood shouted as he kick-started the engine and began to drive off down the hill towards Scallywag Bay, Watson hanging onto the sidecar for dear life as he did so.

"Let's see what the day has in store for us today shall we?" Sherwood said as the wind whipped past his ears as they sped down the hill, "I wonder who will need our help first this fine morning?"

Just then, Sherwood's police radio noisily buzzed into life which almost caused Watson to jump out of his furry skin.

"PC Holmes, come in, over," said a gruff sounding woman's voice.

Sherwood smiled as he grabbed the receiver, recognising that it belonged to Sergeant Maja from the Scallywag Bay police station.

"Morning Sherwood," the police sergeant said, "hope you had a good night's sleep, over."

"Wasn't too bad, Sarge," Sherwood replied, "would have been so much better if Watson hadn't snored so much though, over."

Sherwood looked at his faithful cat who bowed his head down sheepishly.

"Sorry to hear that, Sherwood," Sergeant Maja replied, "unfortunately we've a few house calls we'd like you to make before you come into the station today, over."

"No problems, Sarge, let me get my notebook," Sherwood smiled, taking a large mouthful of coffee before reaching into his pocket, "right then, fire away…"

Chapter Two

The first call Sergeant Maja asked Sherwood to make was to go and see Sue Magoo at number 52 which was not that far from Sherwood's house.

It only took Sherwood and Watson a couple of minutes to reach the quaint, little cottage not far from where they both lived on the outskirts of the town.

"You stay here, Watson," Sherwood said as he made his way down the path, "this shouldn't take me too long."

Watson mewed and yawned as Sherwood knocked three times on the old wooden door.

Knock...

Knock...

Knock...

"No need to knock the door, down! Just give me a minute…" cried a woman's voice, "I've lost my glasses not my hearing! Hang on a second, I've got to feel my way there instead!"

Sherwood smiled to himself as he listened to the loud bangs and crashes which came from inside the cottage before the front door finally opened.

"Hello, who's there?" a little old lady said, her face screwed and scrunched up as she squinted at Sherwood.

"PC Holmes, Mrs Magoo," Sherwood smiled, "you called the station earlier this morning.

"Oh, thank you, thank you, miss," Sue Magoo said, "please come in."

Sherwood sighed and watched as Sue Magoo stumbled back towards her kitchen, bumping into all of her furniture, swearing loudly, before she eventually stood next to her kitchen sink.

"So, what seems to be the problem, Mrs Magoo?" Sherwood asked, taking out his notebook.

"When I came into the kitchen this morning to fill up the kettle," Sue Magoo replied, nodding at the window, "someone was outside staring back at me."

"Oh, dear me," Sherwood replied, licking the tip of his pencil before writing, "and when was this exactly?"

"Just before sunrise," Sue Magoo said, "I remember thinking to myself 'who could it be lurking about it the dark so early in the morning.'"

"What did you do next?" Sherwood asked.

"I grabbed my broom and went outside to chase them off of course!" Sue Magoo said, "but when I got out there, they were gone so I came back inside again. But guess what?"

"What?" Sherwood said, furiously scribbling away on his notebook.

"There they were - back at the window," Sue said, "staring right back at me again, the cheeky so and so. That's when I called the station."

"How odd…" Sherwood replied, staring out the window into Mrs Magoo's garden before flipping over another page in his notebook, "Do you think you could describe them to me please?"

"I'll try but my eyesight isn't as good as used to be," Sue Magoo sighed, "and, as I've already said, I've lost my blessed glasses."

Sherwood stood with his pencil poised, ready to write her description down as Sue Magoo scratched her head and sighed.

"Let me see now…they were short, probably about the same height as me," she said, adding, "with curly, grey hair, like mine. They were also wearing something draped over their shoulders, a dark colour I think…"

"Short…curly grey hair…something over their…" Sherwood repeated before stopping the note he was writing, "could they have been wearing a shawl like the one you have on today, Mrs Magoo?"

"Hmmm, yes, I suppose it could have been a shawl," Sue Magoo frowned, "it was just so dark that it was really hard to tell."

"You say that saw them just before sunrise," Sherwood said, putting his notebook away before opening the cottage door and stepping outside.

"Yes," Sue Magoo replied, "I remember thinking to myself who on Earth would be out about so early as the sun had yet to come up, Constable Holmes."

"And would you recognise this person again if you ever saw them," Sherwood shouted as he made his way around to the garden in front of the kitchen window, unbuttoning his police tunic as he did so.

"Definitely," Sue Magoo said, peering out the window to see what Sherwood was doing, "I never forget a face once I've seen it."

"I'm sure you don't, Mrs Magoo," Sherwood said as he held his police tunic up against the window.

He looked across at Watson who was still patiently sat in the sidecar and began to quietly count to himself.

"One…two…thr-"

"Constable Holmes…Constable Holmes…" screamed Sue Magoo, "Oh where's that young lady now…? They're back outside my window! Oh, I wish I could find my glasses so that I can see who that cheeky beggar really is! I'll give them a good piece of my mind when I finally get my hands on them, just you wait and see…"

Chapter Three

After eventually managing to convince Sue Magoo that her mystery visitor was none other than her own reflection, Sherwood and Watson were soon on their way again, carefully winding their way around the cobbled streets and narrow lanes of Scallywag Bay.

"Got to now go and investigate a complaint that's been made about a nuisance neighbour next, Watson," Sherwood said as he slowly turned a sharp corner on his motorcycle as they made their way up Victory Hill.

Suddenly, from out of nowhere, another vehicle quickly appeared on his side of the road. "Whoa!" Sherwood shouted as he quickly moved his motorcycle out of the way, Watson putting his paws over his eyes as the other motor vehicle sped past them, narrowly missing both of them by inches, much to their relief.

Sherwood stopped his motorcycle, put the brake on

and turned to get a good look at the driver of the other strange and unusual vehicle.

"What on Earth…" he gasped, suddenly realizing that the mystery driver appeared to be riding two motorized E-scooters which were strapped on either side of a large walking frame which the driver held on to in the middle of them.

"Looks like house call number two will have to wait a little longer today, Watson," Sherwood shouted as he began to turn his motorcycle around to chase the strange E-scooter rider who was now rapidly disappearing back down the hill towards the sea front.

But before Sherwood had even managed to do so, a rickety old mobility scooter, ridden by someone much smaller, wearing a bashed and battered mirrored old helmet, went zooming past him. "Out of my way," a gruff Scottish voice shouted, "I've finally got that cheating bounder in my sights!"

Watson rubbed his eyes with his paws as he and Sherwood watched as the mobility scooter bounced over the and weaved its way down the hill in search of the e-scooter/walking frame hybrid vehicle which had turned the corner which led down to the sea front just a matter of seconds before. "Right, hold on Watson," Sherwood said as he gunned his engine again, "trust me, those two speed demons are not going to get away with this…

It only took Sherwood a matter of minutes to make his way back down the hill on his motorcycle - with Watson safely strapped in beside him - and onto the long Victorian seafront which Scallywag Bay was world famous for.

Up ahead, Sherwood could clearly make out the two racers as they sped away from him, the mobility scooter quickly gaining ground on the weird e-scooter/walking frame contraption which was rattling along in front of him.

"Mew, mew, mew, mew," Watson said as the sea

wind rippled his long, furry ears.

"Don't you worry about that, old friend," Sherwood smiled, "it will only be a matter of time before we catch up with them both – see?"

Watson looked up to see that the seafront ahead of them had been closed due to a huge landslip during a huge summer storm a few weeks earlier which had covered the road, stopping both racers in their tracks.

By the time that Sherwood and Watson reached them, they had both removed their helmets and were fiercely arguing with one another.

"You only managed to catch up with me, Will, because I couldn't go any further along the front and had to stop," an elderly man standing next to the e-scooter was saying as he waved his hands at the much smaller man still sat on the mobility scooter in front of him.

"What utter nonsense, you old fool," the old man snarled, "I would have whizzed past you in seconds,

Max, just like I used to in the old days…"

"What rubbish? How many times were you the world champion, Will? Two…three?" the elderly man called Max spluttered, "Last time I counted, I'd won five more titles than you!"

"That's only because I retired before you did," Will replied, "otherwise you'd have won a lot less because of me, you Sunday driver you!"

Sherwood sighed as he walked up to the two men who were now pushing and shoving one another about, tottering around on their feet.

He'd already heard lots about the bitter rivalry of William Speed and Maxwell Power, the two retired Formula 1 world motor racing champions who now lived at the Rest Easy Care Home, from his friends at the police station but had yet to actually see it in person himself.

"Gentlemen, please calm down," Sherwood said as he gently pushed the two men apart, "it doesn't matter who is or was the better driver, you can't use the streets of Scallywag Bay as your own private racetrack!"

"Well, he started it," huffed Max, "always bragging about how he's the greatest motor racing driver who's ever lived."

"That's because it's true!" snapped Will, "the only thing you're good at driving at is people round the bend!"

Sherwood shook his head as he listened to the two men continue to bicker and gripe, wondering how on Earth he would ever get them to stop.

He looked back at Watson, who was still sat with his paws over his ears, in the motorcycle sidecar which Sherwood had parked outside of Scally Island Amusement Land. Sherwood smiled and waved at Roly Coaster, the amusement park owner stood by the entrance, who then smiled and waved back at him.

"Gentlemen," Sherwood smiled, turning back to the angry pensioners, "please will you both follow me.

I think I may have found a much safer way for you to settle your argument with one another, once and for all…"

Chapter Four

"Where are they both now, Sherwood? Over." Sergeant Maja asked as Sherwood finally stood outside one of the three terraced houses in Railway Sidings where his second call of the day was.

"Last I saw of them," Sherwood said speaking into the walkie talkie radio he held in his hand, "they were bashing seven bells out of one another on the dodgems, over,"

"And you're sure Roly doesn't mind having them there all day? Over."

"Absolutely not," Sherwood replied, knocking on the door with his free hand, "he says they can use them for as long as they like, over."

"Why's that then? Over," Sergeant Maja asked as the sound of heavy footsteps began to approach the door Sherwood was stood before.

"Because it makes it looks like Scally Island's dodgems are always busy when they're not so others might want to visit the amusement park too," Sherwood replied as the heavy door swung wide open, "anyway, gotta dash Sarge – I've finally made it to my second house call, over."

"Good luck – I think you're going to need it with that one, over," Sherwood thought he heard Sergeant Maja chuckle as the door swung open to reveal a bald-headed man wearing a fluffy white dressing gown.

"Mr Cheema?" Sherwood asked as a pug appeared at the door beside its owner, "PC Holmes, Scallywag Bay Police."

The small dog growled at Watson sat in the sidecar. Unfazed, the large cat loudly hissed back, causing the pug to yelp loudly and run back inside as the man stuck out a hand.

"Please call me Tariq, PC Holmes," Tariq Cheema replied as he firmly shook Sherwood's hand, "thank goodness you're here. Please do come in."

Sherwood followed Tariq Cheema into the small,

terraced building as he continued.

"I was so worried that you weren't coming," Tariq Cheema said as the two of them walked into a small living room which had a large conservatory at the far end of it, "my Gordan's been at his wit's end with all the nonsense that's been going on around here this morning."

"Oh, I'm very sorry to hear that," Sherwood said, bending down to stroke the pug who was now cowering behind the sofa, "can't have Gordan the dog all upset now, can we?"

"Not Gordan the dog..." a loud voice boomed behind Sherwood, "Gordan the husband...me!"

Sherwood stood bolt upright to find himself staring into the eyes of a huge man who now towered over him.

"I'm ever so sorry, sir," Sherwood smiled, feeling slightly embarrassed as Gordan Cheema linked arms with his husband and sniffed angrily.

"Well, you took your time, didn't you?" Gordan

Cheema snorted, "we could have both died of the shock by the time you finally got here."

"Now dear, don't exaggerate," Tariq Cheema smiled, patting his partner's arm gently, "I'm sure the officer had other more urgent matters he had to attend to first."

"Unfortunately, I did," Sherwood replied, taking his notebook out of his pocket, "but I'm here now, so what seems to be the problem."

"It's *her* again," Gordan hissed, "I'm not sure how much longer I can put up with *her* and her…her…antics!"

Sherwood looked up and frowned. "Are you talking about the nuisance neighbour you reported to the station this morning."

"Yes, that's correct," Tariq Cheema smiled, "Miss Moody who lives next door to us."

Sherwood began to make notes as Tariq Cheema continued. "We've lived here for five years and never had a single problem with any of our previous neighbours…"

"At least, not until that Moody woman moved in two months ago," Gordan Cheema interrupted, "since then we've had nothing but problems with her and her ridiculous beliefs."

"Beliefs…" Sherwood said seriously, suddenly looking up from his notebook, "just exactly what sort of *beliefs*?"

"Come see for yourself," Gordan Cheema tutted, striding into the glass windowed conservatory that looked out across a huge garden which stretched the length of the railway bank in the near distance.

"I hope you're not easily shocked," Tariq Cheema smiled as he and Sherwood followed.

"Trust me, Mr Cheema, I've not," Sherwood replied as he followed Tariq into the conservatory before looking out the window, "after all, I am a police off…oh my word! I so did not expect to see that!"

"Not the sort of view one would expect when eating your coco pops first thing in the morning, would you not agree?" Gordan Cheema sighed as Sherwood rubbed his eyes in disbelief at the sight of the naked woman who was running around the garden.

"PC Holmes, please allow me to introduce to you to Trudy Moody," Tariq Cheema sighed, "our nudie next door neighbour…"

Having heard how Trudy Moody had first nakedly terrified Miss Snuggles – Tariq and Gordan's pug – by doing star jumps in the garden, Sherwood tried hard to hide his smile as Gordan Cheema explained how upset he was when he saw her doing her high knees exercises afterwards.

"I felt quite queasy when I first saw her do them," he explained, "her wobbly bits were flying about everywhere."

"And then when she bent down to touch her toes," Tariq added, "it was like watching a total eclipse of the sun!"

Sherwood closed his notebook and looked up, just

in time to see Trudy Moody striding back into her house.

"Well, I think it's high time that I had a word with Miss Moody," Sherwood said, turning for the front door.

"Are you going to arrest her?" Gordan asked, "After all, being naked outdoors is a crime, isn't it?"

"Actually, public nudity is not an offence, Mr Cheema," Sherwood replied, "and, technically, she is in her own garden so she could claim that she is causing no harm to others."

Sherwood could tell by the way the colour was changing in Gordan Cheema's face that he was about to explode with anger so he raised his hands to calm him.

"However," Sherwood added, "as she may be causing you harm or distress, I'll first have a quiet word with her and ask her to be more discreet in future."

Gordan Cheema went to argue again but was soon

stopped by his husband who gently put his hand on his shoulder.

"Thank you, officer," Tariq Cheema smiled, "we hope that she sees reason after speaking to you…"

However, if Sherwood thought that Gordan Cheema was difficult to deal with, Trudy Moody proved to be even more unreasonable when she answered her front door to him.

"No, I will not put some clothes on when I exercise!" she huffed, "it's a free country and I have every right to follow my beliefs. After all, *'an Englishman's home is his castle'* as they say."

"You're quite right, Miss Moody," Sherwood replied, doing everything he could to avoid looking at the naked woman now stood before him, "being a naturist isn't against the law but offending your neighbours with your nudity is.

"How dare they complain!" Trudy Moody moaned, "Do I complain about them being gay?"

"That's because they are doing nothing to offend you, are they?" Sherwood sighed, "Besides, there's absolutely nothing wrong with them being gay now, is there?"

"Well, there absolutely nothing wrong about exercising in the nude either," Trudy huffed, "it's the way God intended us all to be."

"Yes, but God didn't intend for you to wave your naked bottom in front of your neighbours' window now, did he?" Sherwood firmly replied, adding, "Therefore, I must insist that you stop doing so immediately."

Sherwood reluctantly turned to look at Trudy Moody, fixing his eyes on hers, ready to continue arguing but was surprised to see her frown and nod her head sadly.

"I suppose you're right, officer," she replied, crossing her arms across her chest, much to Sherwood's relief, "it's just that I have been trying to get myself fit again and feel so much better when doing so out in the open. Looks like I'll have to make do with trying to keep fit on my exercise bike indoors instead…"

"Perhaps not," Sherwood smiled, a bright idea suddenly coming to mind, "may I borrow your phone please, Miss Moody?"

"Of course you can, officer," Trudy Moody replied, turning to make her way down the hallway, "this way."

"Thank you," Sherwood said as he followed the naturist into her house, his eyes firmly glued to the floor as his did so…

Once Sherwood got to the old-fashioned phone mounted on Trudy Moody's kitchen wall, he picked up the handset and began to dial.

"Who are you calling, may I ask, constable?" Trudy Moody asked.

"The town hall," Sherwood smiled, "there might be a way for you to still do your exercises out in the open the way you want, as well as helping out the council at the very same time…"

Sherwood felt quite pleased with himself.

After speaking to Sandy Shores, the council officer in charge of Scallywag Bay's beaches, Sherwood had driven Trudy Moody – the naturist wearing nothing but a crash helmet and goggles - in his sidecar down to the other end of the town whilst Watson had happily stayed with Tariq and Gordan Cheema.

When the two of them arrived at the quiet and private beach known as Skinnydip Cove, Trudy's eyes lit up.

"One of Scallywag Bay's best kept secrets," Sherwood smiled as Trudy Moody leapt out of the sidecar and ran to join several other people who were happily enjoying the early morning sunshine whilst all being in the altogether.

"How marvellous!" Trudy Moody laughed as she was greeted by the others – men and women of all ages, shapes and sizes who all had one thing and one thing only in common…

Not one of them was wearing a single stitch of clothing!

"I remembered something Sandy Shores told me at five-a-side football last week," Sherwood called after her, "he said that the Skinnydip Cove Naturist Club were struggling to find a fitness instructor. I thought that it might be something that you'd like to volunteer to do."

"Absolutely!" Trudy grinned, picking up a beach ball that had rolled towards her before happily throwing it back to its grateful owner,

"They have a bus that collects all the town's naturists at 6 am every day," Sherwood shouted as Trudy Moody smiled and waved back at him. "It will then take you all home again two hours later," he added.

"How can I ever thank you, officer?" Trudy Moody shouted as a cheery looking woman invited her to join her and her friends.

"No need to thank me, Miss Moody," Sherwood said as he slowly began to drive away, "just remember not to moon your neighbours anymore in future!"

Chapter Five

It took quite a few minutes for Sherwood to convince Watson to leave the warmth of the Cheemas' sun-filled conservatory before the two of them were finally on their way to the police station in the middle of Scallywag Bay.

"Three house calls completed already this morning, and it's not even nine o'clock yet!" Sherwood said, "so much for it being peaceful and quiet out in the countryside, eh Watson?"

"Mew, mew, mew," Watson mewed, slowly shaking his head.

"You're absolutely right, old boy," Sherwood replied, "I shouldn't moan. It's our job to help people, isn't it? Come on, let's head down to the station to see what else there is in store for us today."

The two of them had travelled no more than a few hundred metres before Sherwood's police radio began to loudly buzz once more.

"No rest for the wicked, eh?" Sherwood sighed as he slowed his motorcycle down before stopping by side of the road.

"Come in, Sarge, over." he said, lifting his walkie talkie to his ear.

"Ah, Sherwood, sorry to be the bearer of bad news," Sergeant Maja said, her voice crackling over the old police radio, "I'm sorry to have to ask but before you finally come into the station today, I've one more urgent house call I need you to make."

Sherwood gave a big sigh but smiled. "Of course, Sarge, it's my job after all. Where do you want me to go to now? Over."

"Thanks, Sherwood," Sergeant Maja replied, quickly adding," I need you to call in to see Patty Cake at her bakery, over."

"Are you still feeling a bit peckish after your breakfast by any chance, Sarge?" Sherwood laughed, remembering that Sergeant Maja had a very, very sweet tooth, "Want me to pick you up a bag of donuts or something? Over."

"I wish it was a simple as that Sherwood," Sergeant Maja said sadly, "no, unfortunately it seems that there was a robbery there late last night, over."

"Oh dear, oh dear," Sherwood replied, "poor Patty. I'll get over there right away, over."

"Thanks, Sherwood," Sergeant Maja replied, adding, "whilst you're there though, I suppose you could always pick me a bag of donuts, just as evidence of course, over."

"Will do, Sarge, over and out," Sherwood said as he pulled his goggles down over his eyes, "Hold on to your hat, Watson, looks like we've got yet another problem to solve today."

"Mew, mew, mew, mew, meeeeeeew," Watson yawned as he pulled his googles back down over his eyes.

"You're absolutely right, old friend," Sherwood replied, turning his motorcycle around again, "a police constable's job is never done…"

And with that the two of them sped back down the hill towards the sun covered town, the waves of the sea gently lapping its golden shores in the distance.

Chapter Six

When they finally arrived at Patty Cake's bakery just off Dumpling Street, they found the front door wide open and her side window broken.

"Hello there," Sherwood called, climbing off his motorcycle, Watson quickly scrambling after him.

Slowly, they both popped their heads around the door to find Scallywag Bay's finest baker Patty Cake sat at the table in the back of her bakery, sadly looking at the mess that had been made by whoever had broken in the night before.

When she saw both Sherwood and Watson her face quickly brightened.

"Oh, am I glad to see you, Sherwood" she sighed, "just look at state of my bakery. Who would do such a terrible thing?"

"That's what we're here to find out," the police constable said as he walked around the bakery, a large magnifying glass gripped in his hand, Watson closely following behind sniffing the floor, his long tail pointing high into the air.

"What's Watson doing?" Patty asked, "Is he looking for clues too?"

Sherwood frowned and shook his head.

"Knowing Watson, he's probably searching for any scraps of food he can find! He's like a giant walking stomach!" he laughed, "I've never known a moggy who's more dog than cat!"

"Mew, mew!" Watson protested, grumpily sitting in the corner.

"And the same to you!" Sherwood replied before turning back to Patty who sat with her arms resting on the table.

"Are you able to tell me anything about what's happened here then Patty?" Sherwood asked, grabbing his pencil and notebook for what seemed to have been the umpteenth time that day.

Patty sighed, sniffed and shook her head sadly.

"I can't really tell you much more than what you can

already see for yourself, Sherwood," the baker said, "I turned up a little late for work this morning to open the bakery and found the side window broken and the front door wide open."

"Hmm…" Sherwood said, crouching to look at a single smudged and floury footprint on the wooden floor, "Looks like they broke in through the window at the side and then left by opening the front door and running through it. Tell me, was there much taken?"

"Fortunately, I banked all our money yesterday afternoon," Patty replied, "however, whoever did this cleared out my entire pantry and stockroom as well as my two fridges. Just look at the mess they've left my bakery in though!"

"Mew, mew, mew, mew, mew," Watson purred, licking his tail in the process.

"I was just about to get to that, Watson," Sherwood sighed as he turned back to Patty, "as my very good friend here has just asked me, exactly what did they steal from you, Patty?

"Pretty much my entire stock," Patty replied, waving her hand around her, "all my milk, caster sugar, butter, eggs, plain and self-rising flour to name but a few things…"

Sherwood nodded as he scribbled down his notes, desperately trying to keep up with Patty Cake as she continued to list the items which had been stolen from her bakery.

"Yeast, baking powder, baking soda," Patty added, counting the items lost on her fingers and thumbs, "honey, syrup, all my spices, vegetable oil, lard, chocolate chips, sprinkles and much, much more!"

"Fortunately, they're all things which can easily be replaced by your insurance," Sherwood replied before he quickly added, "you do have insurance for your bakery, don't you, Patty?"

"Of course, I do, Sherwood!" Patty sniffed.

"Then look on the bright side, Patty," Sherwood smiled, "if we don't catch the rascal and find your missing goods straight away, at least it won't be too long before you'll be able to use the money that you'll get from the insurance to stock up once again."

"And normally that would be OK, though rather annoying that I'd have to do that in the first place…" Patty grumbled before quickly adding, "However, I've a really big order I was going to have to put together today…"

Sherwood pulled out a chair and sat down at a table opposite Patty as she told him about the party she'd been asked to bake for the following day.

"Mr Read and Miss Wright from Scallywags School have ordered fifty large cakes to be delivered by two o'clock tomorrow afternoon," Patty explained, "it's Scally the Wag's Bank Holiday weekend so as well as celebrating that, the school will be holding both their summer fete and a surprise farewell party for their head teacher who retired yesterday."

"You're going to be awfully busy today then, aren't

you, Patty?" Sherwood smiled, nodding at Watson to follow him, "so why don't you leave the two of us to try and find all your missing goods. In the meantime, you can then concentrate on contacting all your suppliers to get everything you need to complete your order for tomorrow."

Sherwood went to leave but could tell by the sad look on Patty's face that something still wasn't quite right so sat back down again at the table.

"If it were only that simple, Sherwood," Patty sniffed, wiping away a tear which had escaped her eye, "As I said, it's Scally the Wag's Bank Holiday weekend…all my suppliers, as well as all the shops and stores around Scallywag Bay are shut for the weekend as tomorrow is Scally's Day itself."

"Of course," Sherwood replied, remembering that Sergeant Maja had told him shortly after arriving from London that the whole of Scallywag Bay and the surrounding villages ground to a halt once a year to celebrate the day when the famous Viking invader - Scally the Wag - first invaded the beautiful county now known as Blinkingshire back in 865AD, immediately founding and naming the bay after himself.

"What on Earth am I going to do, Sherwood?" Patty moaned, holding her head in her hands, "there's absolutely no way I'll be able to replace all the ingredients I need in time to complete my order."

"There, there, don't you worry, Patty, we'll sort something out." Sherwood said smiling. "tell you what, let's help you get tidied up here first and then we can see what can be done to help you."

"Thank you, Sherwood," Patty smiled, you really are too kind."

As Sherwood and Patty began to clear up the broken glass, right the furniture and sweep the floors, across Dumpling Street, the Jones twins – Charlie and Holly – were passing by the bakery on their way up to Scallywags School.

When they saw Sherwood's motorcycle, their eyes

lit up at the thought that their favourite police officer, who they had first met when he came into school earlier that year, was nearby.

"The door to Patty Cake's bakery is wide open," Charlie said to his sister, "maybe he's in there talking to her about something or other."

"Well, there's only one way to find out..." Holly replied, bounding across the street, her ever-so-slightly younger twin chasing after her.

Slowly, they popped their heads around the door of the bakery.

"Hello PC Holmes," they said together in perfect harmony.

"Hello Charlie...Holly," Sherwood replied, setting a chair back on its feet, "fancy seeing you both here so bright and early. I'd have thought that you two would have been enjoying a long lie-in today, especially as it's the first day of the summer holidays."

"Normally we would, PC Holmes," Holly smiled,

"but we're on a special mission at our school today."

"Sounds very mysterious," Sherwood replied, "are you able to tell me what it is?"

"It'll cost you a ride in your sidecar!" Charlie said cheekily, his sister giggling naughtily beside him.

"Deal!" Sherwood replied, winking at Patty who seemed to welcome the distraction of the children's arrival.

"Mr Learner, our headmaster, has just retired," Holly began to explain, "so our class have been helping to arrange his leaving party with Mr Read and Miss Wright for tomorrow as part of the Scally's Day celebrations."

"There's going to be stalls and stands, as well as a bouncy castle and lots of other fun things for all the family to do," Charlie added, "there's also going to be a huge food tent so that we can have our very own Scallywag Bay Bake Off…"

"That's how we've all tricked Mr Learner to definitely be there tomorrow," Holly grinned, "he thinks he's just coming by to judge who has made Scallywag Bay's best cake this year."

"Except for the fact that all of the cakes he'll be judging will have been made by Patty for his surprise party," Charlie added, smiling at the baker, "we can't wait to see the look on his face when…"

The sight of Patty Cake bursting into tears caused Charlie Jones to stop in his tracks as Watson rubbed against the baker's legs, trying hard to console her.

"Sorry, Patty," Charlie said, "did I say something to upset you?"

"No, you didn't Charlie," Sherwood replied, handing the young baker his handkerchief, "you see, Patty has had a rather bad morning so far…"

Charlie and Holly listened in horror as Sherwood told them all about the robbery and the problems that Patty would now face trying to have all of the cakes baked and ready for the party the very next day.

"So, you see, kids," Sherwood said finally, "we're

in a quite a bit of a pickle here this morning."

Holly started to shake her head as she turned to look at her brother before her eyes were lit up by an idea. "What if we help you to go around all of the houses in Scallywag Bay," she said, "and ask for any spare ingredients anyone might have to help you make all the cakes needed."

"What a great idea," said Sherwood, "it's got to be worth a try, hasn't it, Patty?"

"Yes, it does, I suppose," Patty frowned, "but didn't you say that you were on your way to school to help out there? By the time you're done, it will be too late for me to cook all the cakes needed."

"We'll go hunting around the village first then we'll go to school," smiled Charlie, "there will be plenty of our school friends already there, so we won't be missed too much."

"Plus, we can always go and help out there once we've finished helping you here, can't we?" Holly added.

Sherwood grinned as he watched Patty's face beam for the first time that morning.

"That's so very kind of you both," Patty smiled before a frown crept back onto her face, "but it will take you ages to go around everyone's houses."

"Not if PC Holmes gives us that ride on his motorcycle and sidecar like he promised," laughed Charlie, winking at Sherwood.

"Well, I can't exactly say no now, can I?" Sherwood replied, adding, "I'll just phone the station to tell them that this case is taking longer than expected and then we'll be on our way. Patty, you ride a scooter, could we borrow your helmet for one of the twins, I'll lend Watson's to the other."

"Of course," Patty replied, "it's the very least that I can do…"

As the baker rushed off to find her helmet to give to Sherwood, the police constable bent down to where Watson lay on the floor, enjoying the belly rub Charlie was now giving him.

"Now, you wait here, Watson, I'm pretty sure that Patty won't mind you keeping her company," Sherwood said, "you never know, she might find the odd crumb or two still for you to help her clear up."

"Mew-mew," Watson replied, licking his lips.

"You're telling me that it's a dirty job, but someone has to do it!" Sherwood laughed as Patty returned to hand him her scooter helmet, "Thanks Patty. Now, can you make us a list of all the things you need us to find for you."

Sherwood passed Patty his notebook and pencil and watched as the baker quickly scribbled down her wish list of ingredients before giving it back to him.

"Right then, you two," Sherwood smiled, giving a helmet each to Charlie and Holly, "pop these on. Then we'll be on our way."

"Good luck," Patty called as the three of them made their way out of the bakery door.

"First one there gets to ride in the sidecar," Holly shouted, having already begun to run towards

Sherwood's motorcycle.

"Not fair!" Charlie moaned as he watched his sister jump into the sidecar before he'd even managed to break into a run.

"Don't worry, Charlie," Sherwood smiled, handing the young boy his notebook, "you can keep track of what we need, as well as riding behind me on the back of the motorcycle."

Charlie stuck his tongue out at his sister as he climbed onto the motorcycle seat behind Sherwood, tearing the list from the notebook and pinning it to the back of Sherwood's tunic with the prefect badge he was wearing.

"Brilliant thinking, Charlie," Sherwood smiled as he pulled on his gloves and lowered his goggles over his eyes.

"Elementary, my dear PC Holmes!" Charlie chuckled before wrapping his arms around the police constable's waist.

"Hold on tight, kids!" Sherwood shouted as he

revved the motorcycle's engine, "It might be a bit of a bumpy ride…"

"Will we have enough room to carry all that we need?" Holly asked as they began to make their way along Dumpling Street.

"No," Sherwood said, "so we might have to go back and forth quite a bit today."

"Cool," Charlie smiled, "then we can take it in turns to sit in the sidecar, right sis?"

Holly nodded as they approached the end of the street. From the doorway of her bakery, Patty and Watson watched and waved as Sherwood and the children motored off, carrying all of the young baker's hopes with them…

Chapter Seven

As Sherwood slowly wound his way around the narrow streets and lanes which led away from Dumpling Street, Charlie and Holly grinned happily as they watched the beauty of Scallywag Bay pass them by, excited to finally be riding a motorcycle and sidecar…

PC Holmes' motorcycle and sidecar…

"Right then, Charlie," Sherwood shouted to make his voice heard over the spluttering engine, "what does the list say we need first?"

Charlie peered at the list pinned to Sherwood's back, trying to make out the words written on it as they bounced up and down on the cobbles.

"Flour," Charlie replied, "lots of flour."

"Plain or self-raising?" Sherwood asked as he leant the bike into a sharp corner, Charlie and Holly copying his movements exactly.

"Self-raising flour," Charlie shouted as the chalky,

white sea cliffs started to come into view.

"Where would be the best place to get enough of that from, I wonder?" Sherwood said, turning another sharp corner so that the sea cliffs were now on the other side of them.

"I know," said Holly, "why don't we go see if Max Miller is at his windmill this morning? Even though it's a bank holiday weekend, I'm sure he'd want to help."

"What a great idea" said Sherwood, turning left off the main road to head in the direction of the only working windmill in Blinkingshire – Max Miller's windmill which stood at Miller's Crossing...

When they eventually got there, they found Max sat in the yard, covered from head to foot in powdery white dust, a large cogwheel and steel brush in his hands. He smiled and waved as he watched Sherwood and the children pull up just inside the gates to his yard.

"It's a bit early for Halloween, Max," Sherwood

laughed, "you look just like a ghost out of Scooby Doo!"

"If only..." Max smiled, lifting the cogwheel high in the air, "no, as it's a bank holiday, I thought that I'd use my free time today to clean out the milling machines."

Max slowly stood up and wiped his hands on the front of his overalls. "What brings the three of you out this way this fine summer's morning?"

Sherwood, Charlie and Holly explained to Max what had happened at the bakery and how they were trying to help Patty get all the ingredients she needed for her order.

"We were wondering if you could spare us some self-raising flour?" Holly finally asked.

"Of course I can," said Max, "how much flour do you need exactly?"

"Lots," Charlie added, "enough to bake at least fifty cakes."

Max shook his head and sighed as he glanced at his

windmill which stood silently behind him, there hardly being a hint of a breeze that morning.

"I'll see what I've got left," he said, "however, a baker from Hogswash bought quite a few bags yesterday so I'll have to see what I can find and will drop off what I've got to Patty right away."

"Thanks, Max," Sherwood smiled, "sorry to take you away from what you were doing."

"Trust me, Sherwood," Max laughed, slapping him on the shoulder, leaving a big floury handprint on his tunic, "any excuse to stop me from cleaning is always a good one!"

"What's next on Patty's list?" Sherwood asked as they raced away from Miller's Crossing, the children now having switched places after Charlie had got to the sidecar ahead of his sister.

"There's two more ingredients that she really most, PC Holmes," Holly said, "milk and eggs."

"Then why don't we all head off down to Farmer

Plowright's," said Charlie, "her farm's not all that far from here."

"Hang on to your hats then, kids," Sherwood shouted as they quickly sped over a small bridge, both of the children's tummies flipping as they flew over it.

"That was just like being on a roller-coaster!" Charlie laughed, "I feel wicked!"

"I feel sick," Holly moaned as the three of them raced along the winding lanes towards Farmer Plowright's farm which stood alone in the near distance.

When they finally arrived at the gates of Ramshackle Meadows, there was no sign of Farmer Plowright or any of her farm workers.

"I wonder where she could be?" said Holly, taking off her goggles and looking around the farm towards the pond which lay at the bottom of it.

Suddenly, from somewhere behind them, there was a loud whirring sound as over the brow of the hill came the jolly farmer, desperately hanging onto a quad bike.

"Quick – get out of the way!" Farmer Plowright shouted, waving her hand in front of her, "This blasted thing is completely out of control...I can't stop...run for your lives!"

Sherwood, Charlie and Holly flung themselves in all directions to avoid Farmer Plowright and her quad bike as she whizzed past them, narrowly missing Sherwood's motorcycle as it raced down the hill towards the pond at the bottom of the farmyard.

"Jump!" Holly shouted at Farmer Plowright but it was already too late as the quad bike sped up and over a small mound of earth at the edge of the pond and flew directly into the centre of it...

Splash!

Geese, ducks and frogs angrily honked, quacked and croaked as the murky pond water flowed around the farmer and her quad bike before eventually settling again as Sherwood and the children rushed to help the poor farmer.

"Are you all right, Farmer Plowright? Did you hurt anything?" Holly shouted as Sherwood took off his shoes and socks, rolling his trousers right up to his knees, before slowly wading through the pond water towards the quad bike.

"Only my pride and my bottom, dear," the ruddy faced farmer grunted as Sherwood reached out his arms to help lift her from the moss-covered vehicle. Carefully, the two of them trudged back through the water, avoiding the angry complaints of the geese, ducks and frogs as they climbed back onto bank of the pond.

"I hate these new-fangled inventions" muttered the soggy farmer, "they're more trouble than they're worth! Bought this blasted thing off a crackpot inventor in Codswallop… *The Farmer's Fabulous Friend'*, he called it – hasn't worked properly since the day I bought it!"

As Farmer Plowright wrung out the mucky water

from her clothes and picked the slimy moss and lily pads from out of her hair, Sherwood and the children told her all about the robbery at Patty Cake's bakery.

"We were hoping that we could get all the milk and eggs we need from you, Farmer Plowright," Sherwood asked as the farmer lifted her sodden hat off her head to release a large bull frog who'd been trapped under it.

Farmer Plowright frowned and shook her head.

"I can help you with the milk you need as I've not yet milked the cattle today," she said, "but I sold the last of my eggs to a young man from Hogswash less than an hour ago."

"Hogswash, you say…?" Sherwood said, "How very interesting…"

"Lovely fellow with bright red hair and a bushy beard," Farmer Plowright added, "said that he'd a last-minute rush order that he'd been asked to do so he bought all the eggs I had this morning."

Sherwood looked at the children and frowned.

"I don't suppose you got his name or address, did you?" he asked, "Perhaps he might be able to spare us the odd egg or two…"

"'Fraid not," Farmer Plowright replied, "he paid in cash and then took them all right away with him."

"Oh dear," Charlie sighed, "what will we do now?"

"Tell you what, kids," Farmer Plowright smiled, "I've plenty of cheese you can have instead. Cheese making is both a hobby and a passion of mine, constable."

"Thanks, Farmer Plowright," Sherwood replied, "but we don't need any cheese."

"You can never not need cheese, constable!" Farmer Plowright chuckled, "Nor can you ever have too much of it. I've lots of different cheeses that you can choose from."

Sherwood went to shake his head but his curiosity – as well as his own love of all things cheesy – finally got the better of him.

"As a matter of interest, Farmer Plowright," Sherwood asked, his tummy now rumbling slightly, "what sort of cheeses do you actually make or have here on your farm?"

"Oh, all sorts, constable," Farmer Plowright beamed, "I've Cheddar, Stilton, Stinking Poacher's Cheese, some specially imported Edam from Holland, Tunworth…

"Tunworth?" Holly asked, "What's that one taste like?"

"Oh, I think you'd like that cheese, my dear," Farmer Plowright smiled, "it's quite robust, but also a little soft and nutty…"

"Just like Farmer Plowright!" Charlie whispered to Sherwood who had to stifle his laughter.

"And of course," Farmer Plowright proudly continued, "not forgetting my very own cheese which is our local specialty – Scallywag Foot!"

Sherwood, Charlie and Holly looked at one another in surprise.

"Scallywag Foot?" Sherwood asked, "I've not heard of that before. What's type of cheese is it?"

"Ah, I think that's the one that you'd like best, constable," Farmer Plowright said as she began to squelch back towards her farmhouse, "it's a cross between cottage cheese and Ricotta but tastes so much better than both of them. I've tonnes of it made and maturing if you'd like to sample a piece."

Charlie and Holly looked pleadingly at Sherwood who smiled and nodded as they began to follow the farmer back to her farmhouse.

"Maybe just a quick bite then before we have to be on our way again," Sherwood said before adding, "tell me though – why did you name it Scallywag Foot, Farmer Plowright?"

"Oh, that's an easy one to answer," Farmer Plowright said, taking off a welly to pour some of the pond water out of it, "it's because the cheese smells exactly the same as my feet do at the end of a long day working on the farm..."

Sherwood and the twins immediately stopped in their tracks and stared at one another, all three of them thinking exactly the same thing.

"My, is that the time?" Sherwood said, looking at his wrist, forgetting that he wasn't wearing a watch that day, "sorry, can't stop, we've got a deadline to meet."

"Oh, really?" Farmer Plowright said as she put her welly back on before continuing, "not to worry, I'll drop some off at Patty's for you with the milk she needs once I've changed out of these soggy, wet clothes."

"I'll look forward to it," Sherwood lied as he and the children climbed back onto the motorcycle and sidecar, "be seeing you then."

Farmer Plowright waved and squelched back to the farmhouse as the three of them set off once again.

"A lucky escape there, eh?" Holly whispered once Farmer Plowright was safely out of earshot."

"Most definitely," Sherwood replied, "though it still

leaves up with a problem regarding all of the eggs that Patty needs."

"What are we going to do then, PC Holmes?" Charlie said as they made their way out through the gates of Ramshackle Meadows.

"There's only one other thing we can do," Sherwood replied as they headed back towards the small seaside town again, "we'll knock on the door of as many houses as we can in Scallywag Bay to see who can spare us the odd egg or two!"

Chapter Eight

The sun was now high in the sky as Sherwood and the twins raced around Scallywag Bay on their great egg chase, Holly now taking her second turn at riding in the sidecar.

They decided to start off at Teresa Green's house right at the top of Cemetery Hill. After hearing what they were needed for, Teresa was more than happy to help out and gave them two large white eggs.

"How are we going to carry them?" asked Holly once they got back to the sidecar.

"I know," replied Sherwood, opening the top box on the back of his motorcycle, "if we turn this upside down, you can carry them in my police helmet."

He handed the police helmet to Holly and placed the eggs in it.

"You wait here, Holly," Sherwood said, "Charlie and I will go and knock on the other houses near Teresa's to see what we can get before we head off down the hill again."

Holly nodded as Sherwood and Charlie dashed back and forth, knocking on the doors of Teresa Green's neighbours, asking if they could spare any eggs. They were in luck, starting well on their great egg hunt, being give one by Bill Poster, a couple each from Pearl Barley and Rick Shaw as well as half a carton from Rose White the florist.

"Wow!" said Charlie, "A whole half dozen!"

"And they're from very happy chickens too," smiled Rose, "so they should taste even better!"

Sherwood and Charlie scampered back to Holly and carefully filled up the police helmet.

"If we carry on at this rate," Holly said, "we're going to fill the sidecar up as well!"

"True," Sherwood replied, taking off his tunic, "but it will be better to have too many eggs than too little now, won't it?"

The twins nodded as Sherwood took off his tunic and gently placed it in the footwell of the sidecar, wrapping it around Holly's feet.

"If you run out of room in the helmet," Sherwood said, mounting the motorcycle again, "place the eggs on my tunic instead. It should be soft yet thick enough to protect them if we drive carefully."

Holly nodded as Sherwood started the engine and started to slowly motor down Cemetery Hill, taking great care going over the potholes in the road so as to not break any of the eggs.

"If we carry on at the rate we've been going, we'll have all the eggs we'll need in no time at all," Charlie smiled as they came across a line of bungalows sitting next to one another.

"Here's hoping," Sherwood smiled as he and Charlie jumped off the motorcycle and began to knock one by one on the cottage doors.

Unfortunately, despite calling at several large houses, they only managed to get one more egg from the painter and decorator Annie Glypta to add to their haul.

It was the same story with the rest of the houses which line the road they visited as they made their way down on Cemetery Hill, only gathering three or four more eggs before they reached the cemetery itself at the bottom.

"Once we've knocked on their door," Sherwood said, nodding to a dark and forbidding house at the end of a long drive next to the cemetery, "we'll take stock of how many eggs we have before we head into town again."

Charlie and Holly looked at each other in horror before shaking their heads.

"No point in going there," Charlie said, swallowing hard, "three old and spooky sisters live there and they don't take too kindly to visitors."

"And even if *'The Merry Widows'* - as they're known around here - had any eggs," Holly added, "I doubt very much that they'd share them with us."

"What makes you say that?" Sherwood asked, again looking at the old, run-down Victorian house which seemed to be the only building on Cemetery Hill not to be bathed in bright sunlight.

"During the pandemic," Charlie said, "no one could get any groceries delivered because all the supermarkets had run out of stock."

"That's because the Merry Widows had bought everything up," Holly added, "and then refused to share them with anyone else, supposedly."

"Since you put it like that," Sherwood said sadly, turning his motorcycle around again, "we'll leave them for the time being. But if, by the end of the day, we've not been given enough eggs, then we'll have to pay them a visit. Deal?"

The twins looked at one another and nodded their heads reluctantly.

"But we stay at the end of the drive whilst you go knock the door," Holly said, "as those three sisters give us the creeps!"

Fortunately, by the time that the three of them had reached Dumpling Street again, they'd had more than enough eggs for Patty, having had far greater success with the houses they'd visited in the town centre.

When they arrived back at the bakery, they found Patty sat at the table, along with another young girl who Sherwood wasn't quite sure if he'd ever met before.

"This is Sue Cheff," Patty said, "she's on her summer break from university and has been helping me in the bakery."

"Pleased to meet you," Sherwood said, shaking the girl's hand.

"Likewise," Sue said shyly, her eyes avoiding his as she nervously hid behind her fringe and looked at the ground.

"Which university are you studying at, Sue?" Holly asked as she carefully placed the helmet of eggs on the table, Sherwood's tunic – the arms tied together to stop all the other eggs falling from it – placed beside the helmet.

"East London," Sue said quietly, "I'm studying law there."

"Law, that's wicked!" Holly grinned, "Are you going to be a lawyer when you finish your degree then, Sue?"

"I'm not sure yet," the young girl replied, "possibly."

"Let me tell you this, Sue," Patty said, "if you decide that law's not for you, you would have no problem getting a job in a bakery!"

Sherwood thought he saw Sue's cheeks flush a little at the compliment.

"So, Sue what brings you to Scallywag Bay then?" Sherwood said, untying the sleeves of his tunic before gently sliding it out from under the eggs.

"I've got an aunt who lives in one of the nearby villages," Sue replied, "and my nan lives in one of the others. They suggested I get a summer job to help ends meet. I was lucky that Patty needed help in the bakery."

"And I was lucky to find you, Sue," Patty smiled, "especially as I'll need your help this afternoon to bake as many cakes as we can for tomorrow's party."

"No problem, Patty," Sue said, picking up an apron and tying it around her waist, "I can stay until about six o'clock but then I have to go. I've promised my aunt that we'll drive to my nan's tonight. We're staying over to celebrate Scally's Day in Bunkum tomorrow. They're having a street party there."

"Sounds fab," Sherwood said, putting his tunic back on again, "so Patty, have you all you need now to be getting on with?"

"Not quite," Patty sighed, "I've all the milk I could ever want, along with some cream Farmer Plowright also donated. I've even got lots of other ingredients people have dropped into me today after hearing about the robbery from you three."

"That's good then," replied Sherwood, "so why have you both got such long faces?"

"Max Miller only had just over half the flour I need," Patty sighed, "which means that I'll only be able to make half the cakes that I promised."

"Surely that's better than nothing," Charlie said, trying to look on the bright side.

"Yes, Patty," Sue agreed, "and if we're really clever, we can cut them into thinner slices so that there's more enough to go around."

"I suppose you're right," Patty said, adding, "right then, best be getting on. Thanks once again for all of your help."

"My pleasure, Patty," Sherwood replied, "lovely to meet you, Sue. Hope to see you again soon."

"You too, PC Holmes," Sue replied, having already turned to walk towards the bags of flour which sat in the corner of the bakery.

"Come on kids, I'll drop you both back home," Sherwood said, turning for the door.

"It's all right, PC Holmes," Holly smiled, "we'd best pop into school first to see if they still need us to help with anything."

"All right then," Sherwood smiled, gently nudging Watson who was asleep in the corner with his foot, "come on, sleepyhead, it's just you and me again. Time to go home."

"Wait, Sherwood," Patty said, turning towards one of her fridges, "I've a small package Farmer Plowright left here for you earlier..."

"No, Patty!" Sherwood said before he realised how desperate he sounded, "Can I leave it here with you for a bit as I've got to go to the station next and I've nowhere to keep it."

"Of course, Sherwood," Patty smiled as she walked the police constable and Watson to the door, "thank you once again. I don't know what I'd have done without all your help and support."

"Just doing my job, Patty," Sherwood smiled as he pulled his goggles down over his eyes.

"Actually, I think you went above and beyond that today, Sherwood," Patty said, gently kissing him on his cheek.

"Isn't that what friends are for?" Sherwood replied, feeling his face grow warmer, "I'll see you at the bake-off tomorrow, Patty. I'll be sure to try one of your cakes."

"And I'll be sure to save you a big slice, Sherwood," Patty smiled as Sherwood mounted his motorcycle, Watson jumping into the sidecar, sliding his head into the helmet Holly had left in there before sitting upright again.

"Mew-mew, mew, mew, mew, mew!" Watson said, a wide grin filling his furry features.

"We're just good friends, Watson," Sherwood said, feeling his face flush again, "and I'm so not blushing – it's just really hot out in the sunshine now!

Sherwood kick-started his motorcycle again and looked in his rear mirror to see Patty still stood on her doorstep waving him and Watson off.

"Mew-mew, mew, mew-mew, mew mew!" Watson

chuckled as they sped off along Pudding Street.

"I do not have a crush on Patty!" Sherwood protested, quickly changing the subject as they headed into town, "time to call into the station, Watson. Let's hope the rest of the afternoon isn't anywhere as busy as our morning has been."

Chapter Nine

Sherwood woke bright and early on Sunday morning feeling fully refreshed after all his efforts the day before.

Having arrived at the station after leaving Patty Cake's bakery that Saturday, Sherwood was delighted to discover he'd already completed his eight-hour shift and was no longer needed for the rest of the day.

"You're on the early shift again tomorrow, Sherwood," Sergeant Maja had said, "so get yourself off home for some much-needed rest. Could be another busy one Sunday with it being Scally's Day and all."

Sherwood had needed no second invitation so had immediately taken himself off home. He'd spent the afternoon first in his garden catching the last rays of the day, Watson sprawled on the deckchair beside him before making himself homemade fish and chips for his tea, Watson pacing the kitchen until he got his very own piece of cod which he quickly wolfed down.

After tea, Sherwood had spent the evening practicing the violin, the only other thing that he had in common with his famous ancestor, Sherlock Holmes. However, he would be the first to admit that his fiddling skills were nowhere near as good as his great-great-great-great uncle's had been, something Watson would definitely agree with, the large cat taking himself off upstairs to his bed, burying his head under his pillow as his owner screeched his instrument long into the night.

"Let's hope it's a much quieter day tomorrow, eh Watson?" Sherwood had tiredly yawned before turning in for the night.

However, his hopes were soon dashed within minutes of his shift starting that Sunday morning.

"Sorry to have to ask you so early, Sherwood," Sergeant Maja had said over the radio, "but could you pop over to the village of Codswallop before you come into the station. There are yet more reports of a gigantic white rabbit chasing people on the green again, over."

"Will do, Sarge, over and out," Sherwood had replied, kick-starting his motorcycle and setting off to make the short trip to Codswallop, Watson safely tucked into the sidecar as usual.

"Looks like Psycho the rabbit has evaded us once again, Watson," Sherwood said as he climbed off his motorcycle and looked at the large but now deserted village green which lay before him.

He walked over to the oak tree in the centre of it and ran his hand over the claw marks on its trunk.

"Were it not for clues like this, Watson, I'd say that the sightings of him were just an urban myth or a local legend," Sherwood said looking around again, "but there's no sign of him anywhere now so we'd best be on our way."

Watson seemed to breathe a huge sigh of relief as

Sherwood then slowly made his way back to his motorcycle.

"PC Holmes to Scallywag Station, come in Scallywag Station, over," Sherwood said into his radio as he sat on his motorcycle again, stroking Watson under the chin as he waited for a reply.

"Hello, Sherwood, what's your position? Over," the familiar voice of Sergeant Maja crackled over the airwaves.

"All clear here, Sarge, looks like we were sent on a wild goose chase," Sherwood said, starting his engine, "or should I say a wild bunny chase, over."

"Thanks for checking though, over," Sergeant Maja replied.

"It's my job, Sarge," Sherwood said, checking his watch, "All being well, I should be with you in about twenty minutes, over."

"I'll put the kettle on ready for…hang on a minute, Sherwood," the sergeant replied, "I've just had a note passed to me… I'm afraid that I'll need you to make another house call before you come in, over."

"No problem, Sarge," Sherwood replied, reaching into his pocket for his notebook and pencil, "What's the address? Over."

Sergeant Maja paused for a moment before answering.

"It's Patty Cake's bakery, Sherwood," the sergeant sighed, "someone's broken into it again…"

Sherwood and Watson found Patty sobbing at her table when they arrived at the bakery a short while later.

"They got in through the side window again," she cried, "I can't have boarded it up well enough last night before I left."

Sherwood looked at the empty cake racks behind Patty, Watson lapping up the crumbs that covered the floor below them.

"Whoever it was took all the cakes I baked yesterday," Patty wailed, "now there's no way I can supply the Scallywag Bay Bake Off. Everybody will think that I've let them down."

"Did they take anything else, Patty?" Sherwood said, gently placing his hand on her shoulder.

Patty shook her head. "They didn't need to this time - the cakes were already baked for them! Why would someone do this to me, Sherwood?"

"I'm not altogether certain," the police constable replied as the sound of feet pounding the cobblestones grew nearer.

Sherwood, Watson and Patty all looked at the door just as Charlie and Holly Jones excitedly ran through it.

"Morning," Holly said happily, "we thought we'd pop in to see if you needed anymore- oh no, not again!"

"I'm afraid so," Sherwood said as he took out his magnifying glass from his pocket and began to closely examine the bakery again.

"Not to worry," Charlie said, "we will just have to

go around the town and grab all the things you need to bake the cakes again, won't we?"

Patty shook her head sadly. "There's no point. I've already used the last of Max Miller's flour to bake the ones that have been stolen. There's none left."

"Then we could help you make something else instead," Sherwood replied, desperately trying to cheer Patty up.

"Like what?" Patty said as Sherwood made his way to the pantry.

"Oh, I don't know," he said, opening the fridge, "I'm sure we'll think of something…"

On the shelf in front of him was a small, white package which had *'For Constable Holmes'* scribbled on it. Sherwood sighed and took out the cheese Farmer Plowright had promised him the day before.

"See," Patty said, joining Sherwood in the pantry, "all I've got left are eggs, milk, caster sugar, chocolate bars and chips as well as some tinned fruit, along with some fresh strawberries and raspberries I brought with me from my allotment this morning. There's no way I can bake the cakes that are needed with those ingredients alone."

She stood and watched as Sherwood nervously prodded at the package in his hand.

"What on Earth is that?" Patty asked as Sherwood gingerly began to unwrap in, Watson and the twins now crammed in the doorway, desperately trying to sneak a peek.

"Some awful, stinky stuff Farmer Plowright said I should try," Sherwood said, removing the material covered cheese out of its cardboard container.

Watson, Charlie and Holly all held their breath and their noses as Sherwood untied the string which held the material together to reveal the yellow, gooey soft cheese contained within it.

"It's called Scallywag Foot," Holly shouted, her voice slightly nasally as she pinched the end of her nose, "because its smells like Farmer Plowright's stinky, welly covered feet."

Patty leant down to smell the cheese before jabbing a finger in it.

"Actually, it doesn't smell all that bad…" she smiled as she stuck her finger in her mouth, "and it tastes really amazing!"

"Really?" Sherwood said, scooping up a small piece of the cheese, "Oh my god – you're right! That's delicious."

"Farmer Plowright says that it's a cross between cottage and Ricotta cheese," Holly said as she and her brother squeezed in through the doorway to try a bit for themselves.

"Only better!" Charlie exclaimed as he licked his lips after tasting it as Sherwood threw a piece at Watson to chase around the kitchen floor before gratefully licking it up.

"A cross between cottage and Ricotta cheese …" Patty repeated, a slight frown now creasing her forehead, "I wonder…"

Sherwood and the twins looked at each other for a moment as Patty silently stood there, tapping her chin with her index finger.

"What are you thinking, Patty?" Sherwood said as he watched the pretty baker's face light up for a moment before frowning again.

"I was thinking that if Farmer Plowright had enough of her Scallywag Foot cheese going spare," Patty said, "then I could make some cheesecakes instead. But then I realised that I don't have enough digestive biscuits so bang goes that bright idea."

"We'll go on another treasure hunt then, Patty," Charlie smiled, "only this time we'll go searching for digestive biscuits!"

"Then we can have a Scallywag Bag Cheesecake Off instead!" Holly said excitedly.

"It's a nice idea," Patty said, shaking her head, "but there's no way there will be enough digestives in Scallywag Bay to make as many cheesecakes as we'll need."

"Then we'll ask for other biscuits too," Sherwood said, "surely you can make cheesecakes using different types of biscuit bases, can't you."

"Yes, I could," Patty nodded excitedly, "see if you can get me some packets of ginger nuts, bourbons, Oreos, Biscoff or malted milk biscuits too!"

"Will do," Sherwood replied, "let the school know that there's been a change of plan. Then call Farmer Plowright and get her to drop off all the Scallywag Foot cheese you need."

Patty nodded happily as Sherwood turned to the twins.

"Come on, kids," he said, striding towards the door, "help me empty the top box on my motorcycle. We've a biscuity-mystery to now solve and we'll need all the room possible!"

Chapter Ten

Sherwood and the twins spent almost an hour driving back and forth through the quiet streets and lanes of the town, knocking on as many doors as they could. However, as the town hall clock struck ten, they looked disappointedly at the measly haul of biscuits.

"Three packs of ginger nuts, two packs of digestives, one packet of Oreos, half a pack of malted milk," sighed Holly, "and a third of a pack of bourbon biscuits."

"Not forgetting the fourteen Biscoff biscuits we got from Granny," Charlie added, "even though most of them have been half nibbled by the mice!"

"It hasn't helped that we've not had a reply from over half of the doors we've knocked on this morning," Sherwood said as he started the motorcycle engine again before they slowly headed down towards the bottom of Cemetery Hill.

"Lots of people must have gone away for Scally's Day," Holly said sadly as they slowly approached the cemetery itself.

"We've let Patty down," Charlie sighed, "there's no one else we can ask now."

"Oh yes there is," Sherwood replied, nodding towards the dark and forbidding house at the end of a long drive next to the cemetery.

The twins looked at one another, swallowed hard and nodded their heads reluctantly as Sherwood slowly drove through the tall iron gates, a stone-carved raven mounted on the top of each gate post.

"Drop us off here like you promised, please, PC Holmes," Charlie asked as Sherwood pulled to a halt.

"We promise to get help if you're not back in ten minutes," Holly added as she scrambled out of the sidecar.

Sherwood shook his head and laughed at the two children as they stood, hand-in-hand, at the side of the drive.

"I'm sure that they are just three very sweet, shy and retiring little old ladies," he said as he slowly began to drive towards the house which now seemed darker than ever before.

"Three crazy, creepy old witches more like..." Charlie muttered as they watched Sherwood and the motorcycle grow smaller the closer he got to the house.

"With a bit of luck, there will be no answer there either," Holly said, "then we can all get the hell out of here!"

Sherwood had no sooner knocked on the battered front door of Banshee Manor, as the huge Victorian house was named, than it opened, its hinges screaming nosily as it did so.

"Yes?" a frail hooked-nosed woman, dressed from head to toe in a long, black dress, asked as she stared up at Sherwood.

"Good morning, Miss…"

"It's Mrs, actually - Mrs Flora Pott," the woman curtly said as two other women, both of a similar age and dressed in a similar way, came to join her, seeming to glide across the chipped and tiled floor of the hall as they did so.

The woman nodded to the women now stood either side of her who grinned their toothless grins at Sherwood as she introduced them both to him.

"And these are my sisters," Mrs Pott added, "Mrs Nora Kettle and Mrs Dora Black."

"Pleased to meet you," Sherwood smiled as a cold wind picked up, causing his skin to break out into goosebumps, "I'm PC Sherwood Holmes."

"How may we help you, Constable Holmes?" Mrs Pott said as her two sisters giggled and whispered to one another behind her back.

"Would you like to come inside for a short while, constable?" Mrs Kettle smiled, a thin line of dribble running down her chin.

"We promise we won't bite!" Mrs Black added, wiping the slobber from her lips.

"I'd love to," Sherwood lied nervously, "but I'm on a bit of a deadline today I'm afraid…"

The three sisters stood and silently listened as Sherwood told them all about the robberies at the bakery and how he and the twins had been driving around Scallywag Bay getting all the ingredients Patty Cake needed.

"Are those the two children over there at the end of the drive?" Mrs Pott said nodding to where Charlie and Holly still stood holding hands in the distance.

"Yes, that's them," Sherwood replied, beginning to understand why the three sisters gave everybody the creeps.

"Oh, they look so cute with their rosy cheeks and plump little faces," Mrs Kettle cackled, scrunching her face as she did so, "I do so love children, sister."

"As do I, sister," Mrs Black nodded excitedly, "they're so scrummy that I could just gobble them all up!"

"Quite…" Sherwood said, suddenly realising that the three sisters reminded him of a character who'd once scared him when watching television as a small boy…the evil child catcher from the old film *Chitty-Chitty Bang Bang*!

Sherwood shivered once again which was immediately noticed by the sisters.

"Are you sure that you won't come inside and into the warm, constable?" Mrs Pott asked.

"The three of us have only just got up this morning and have yet to eat," Mrs Kettle smiled.

"We'd love to have you for breakfast," Mrs Black added.

"No, thank you, perhaps another time," Sherwood replied, taking a step or two back from the door, "but I do have one small favour to ask if I may…?"

The three sisters quietly listened as Sherwood listed all of the biscuits that he and the children had been searching the whole of the town of Scallywag Bay for that morning.

They stood and slowly nodded as one, as though their heads were attached together by string as Sherwood explained how he'd been told that the people of Scallywag Bay thought that the sisters were food hoarders and, therefore, liked to store up all of their groceries.

"And they would be quite right in thinking that, constable," Mrs Pott finally replied, "it's only right and proper we do so, is it not, sister?"

"Yes, sister," Mrs Kettle added, "it means that we'll have more than enough food to spare if there's ever another emergency like the last pandemic, won't we, sister?"

"Absolutely, sister, meaning we'll be able to share what we have with everyone else in Scallywag Bay so that nobody is ever without food again,"

Mrs Black said, turning away from the door.

"Come, sisters," Mrs Pott said, quickly following her, "let us go and get all of the biscuits that this fine constable requires."

"Yes, let's, sister..." Mrs Kettle agreed as she glided off after the other two women, the three of them noiselessly disappearing into their kitchen.

Sherwood stood in a state of shock and disbelief for a few minutes until the three sisters eventually returned, their arms full of all the biscuits he could ever wish for. They helped him to fill both the top box on his motorcycle and his sidecar before standing back on the doorstep again.

"Ladies, I really am speechless," Sherwood said as he sat astride his motorcycle again, "I honestly did not expect you to be so friendly and helpful."

"Unfortunately, we have a bit of a bad reputation around the bay," Mrs Pott sternly replied.

"Owing to the fact that all three of us widows..." Mrs Kettle added.

"But as you can see, constable," Mrs Black smiled toothlessly, "we're not anywhere near as scary as people think we are."

"Well, if there's anything that I can do to ever repay your kindness," Sherwood said as he grabbed the handlebars of his motorcycle, "then please feel free to ask."

The three sisters huddled together for a moment, whispering and giggling with each other before turning back towards Sherwood.

"There is something you could do for us, constable, if you would be so kind…" Mrs Pott smiled, revealing her one, single blackened front tooth as she did so, beckoning for Sherwood to move towards her so that she could quietly whisper in his ear…

After hearing her request, Sherwood had sighed and nodded before saying goodbye.

He turned his motorcycle around and began to slowly walk it away from the house, hearing the three sisters' chatter grow behind him quieter as he headed back up the drive towards the twins…

"What a fine young man, sister…"

"He reminds me so much of my husband, sister…"

"Which one, sister…?"

"My next one, sister…

"Don't be so greedy – you've had three already, sister…"

"So have you, sister…"

"Oops – I've had so many I've actually lost count…"

Charlie and Holly's eyes almost popped out of their heads when they saw all of the biscuits which packed the top box and sidecar.

"Sorry, kids," Sherwood smiled, "I'm afraid there's now not enough room for me to give you both a lift back to Patty's."

"That's all right," Charlie smiled, "we know of a good short cut through the cemetery. If we hurry, we'll end up at the bakery around about the same time that you will."

"That's all right then," Sherwood replied, sitting

astride his motorcycle again before adding, "hang on a minute – I thought you two were scared of the cemetery?"

"We're not scared of the cemetery," Holly replied, nodding towards Banshee House as the three sisters slowly closed the door, "we're scared of them!"

"Oh, they're not so bad once you get to know them three!" Sherwood smiled as he started his engine, "after all, look at all the biscuits they gave us!"

"And they really gave you all of these for free?" Charlie said, running his hand through the dozens of packets wedged into the sidecar.

Sherwood smiled and nodded. "Well, almost free… they did ask me for one tiny, little favour though which I've agreed to do for them…"

Charlie frowned and looked at his sister before they both stared back at Sherwood.

"What sort of *favour*, PC Holmes?" Holly asked worriedly.

"They've asked me to take tea with them on my next

day off," Sherwood said as he slowly began to ride away, "don't worry though - I'll be sure to take a couple of friends from the station with me, just in case…"

Chapter Eleven

Sherwood was surprised to see Charlie and Holly sat on the front step of the bakery as he pulled up on Dumpling Street.

"You weren't lying when you said it was a good short cut, were you?" he laughed as he climbed off his motorcycle.

"No, we weren't," Charlie shrugged, "even though the time we saved is pointless now."

"What do you mean?" Sherwood asked as Patty joined the twins in the doorway.

"They mean that your efforts today have all been in vain, Sherwood," she said sadly, turning to head back into the bakery, "we're going to have to finally admit defeat, I'm afraid."

"But look at all the biscuits I managed to get from the Merry Widows," Sherwood said, scooping up several packets of biscuits into his arms as he quickly followed Patty indoors.

"The twins told me what you've done and I'm really

grateful, honestly," Patty smiled, "but after you left, I phoned Mr Read & Miss Wright at the school like you said to. They already knew about the break-ins and are happy to change the bake-off to a cheesecake-off but only if I can still get there in time…"

Patty then explained that a baker from the village of Hogswash had called them to tell them about the robberies, guaranteeing that he'd be able to get the cakes the school needed to them in plenty of time if Patty couldn't meet her deadline to deliver them.

"So, if I can't get the cheesecakes to them by two o'clock at the very latest for Mr Learner's surprise party at three," Patty said, "then they say that they'll have no other choice but to get the cakes delivered to them by the baker from Hogswash."

"Hogswash, eh…that's only a few minutes' drive away from the school, isn't it?" Sherwood frowned as he looked at his watch as the twins walked back inside the bakery, Watson rubbing up against their legs to welcome them back again.

"Look, it's just gone half-past ten," Sherwood said, looking at the large clock on the wall, "that still gives you a good three and a half hours to prepare the cheesecakes and bake them in those huge ovens of yours."

"If only it were that easy, Sherwood," Patty smiled, shaking her head sadly. "I'll never make that many cheesecakes on my own in that space of time, especially as Sue isn't here to help me at all today."

"But you won't be on your own, will you, Patty?" Sherwood smiled, taking off his police tunic, "We'll help you, won't we kids?"

"Yes, please!" came the twins excited reply.

"Are you absolutely sure?" Patty said, smiling, "That would be wonderful. It'll be tight but with the four of us working together, we'll have a good chance of making it…"

"Mew, mew, mew, mew!" Watson moaned crossly. Patty looked at Sherwood who smiled.

"Watson says the five of us," he grinned, "after all, he's a lot smarter than your average moggy!"

"Correction - the five of us," Patty said, scratching Watson under the chin, "thank you all again."

"Don't mention it," Sherwood said, rolling up his shirtsleeves, "I'll let the station know that I'm on urgent police business here for the next few hours and then we'll get cracking…"

Which is exactly what Sherwood did after coming off the radio having spoken to Sergeant Maja.

Each of them had been given their own role in Patty's cheesecake production line…

Watson would press the button on the microwave to melt the butter…

Holly was given the job of crushing the different biscuits and then mixing them with the butter in separate bowls, one for each different type of biscuit base….

Sherwood was tasked with cracking and whisking all the eggs and Scallywag Foot cheese together before passing the mixture to Charlie who would then mix in the caster sugar…

This then left Patty to put each different cheesecake together at every different stage of the operation before putting them in the oven to bake… …

"Phew!" Sherwood said as Patty put the last of the cheesecakes into her ovens before setting their timers, "all we have to do now is wait for them to bake."

"How long will that take, Patty?" Charlie asked, feeling his tummy begin to rumble."

"Oh, anything up to an hour," Patty replied, "just enough time for us to have a cuppa and a bite to eat."

Patty boiled the kettle, then made them all a sandwich and a hot mug of tea, whilst they sat and stared at the giant ovens.

"Haven't you ever heard the phrase '*a watched cheesecake will never bake!*'" Patty frowned, "Look away now!"

All four of them then quickly turned their chairs and

stools around to eat their lunches, Watson rolling over on the floor where he lay in the ovens' warmth so that he too could not see inside them.

Sherwood, Patty and the twins sat in silence, yawning tiredly as they drank their tea, Sherwood's head nodding a couple of times as his body threatened to fall into an after-lunch food coma.

Fortunately, it wasn't too long before all of the timers on the ovens pinged to say that the cheesecakes were ready. Patty rushed to the ovens and started to get the cheesecake tins out, Sherwood helping too, using his tunic as an extra set of oven gloves as they stacked the cheesecakes onto the shelves of Patty's two tall cake racks which stood against the wall behind them.

"They look perfect," Sherwood smiled, "and we've still over an hour to spare. Plenty of time to get them to the school."

"Not so fast, Sherwood," Patty frowned, "we've still got to decorate them."

"Let's get started then!" Charlie grinned, grabbing a bag of chocolate chips.

"Hold your horses there, cowboy," Patty said, turning on a large fan which hung above the cake racks, "they've got to cool first. Normally I'd put them in the fridge for three or four hours. However, let's hope they'll be cool enough in thirty minutes instead..."

"What shall we do in the meantime?" Holly asked, already bored with having to sit around.

"We get all of the toppings that we'll need to decorate ready and prepared," Patty said, handing out the tinned fruit, the fresh strawberries and raspberries as well as the different bars of chocolate to grate and the chocolate chips to sprinkle.

The four of them busied themselves for the next half-hour, the twins helping themselves to the odd piece of fruit or stray bit of chocolate as Patty kept checking the temperature of the cheesecakes.

"I think they're as cool as I'm ever going to get them

in the time we have left," Patty finally frowned as she and Sherwood started to lay them out in rows on the table.

"Right then, guys," Patty said, spatula and spoon in her hands, "on your marks...get set...decorate!"

Hands, fruit and chocolate flew back & forth across the tables as the four of them whizzed around it whilst decorating the cheesecakes, Watson looking on with great amusement and delight, hoping to catch any tasty morsels which might fall his way...the old cat not being disappointed!

Finally, all the cheesecakes were finished and ready to be boxed up. Patty carefully packed each cheesecake and began to pass them down the human chain that Sherwood, Watson and the twins had made to safely load up the baker's van.

When the van was finally full with all the cheesecakes, Patty closed and locked its doors as Sherwood checked his watch again.

"Quarter to two," he said, "just enough time for you

to get to Scallywags School

"As long as I don't get delayed on the way there," Patty frowned, "usually there are lots of floats out on the streets celebrating Scally's Day so they could slow me down quite a bit."

"Don't worry, I'll make sure nothing gets in your way this afternoon..." Sherwood smiled, "fancy an official police escort to help deliver your cheesecakes, Patty?"

"Oh, you'll be just like the royal family," laughed Charlie as the five of them gathered outside, Watson jumping into the sidecar as the twins climbed into the van besides Patty.

"Ready when you are, Sherwood," Patty laughed as the police constable kick-started his motorcycle before turning on his siren and blue light as the five of them raced off along Dumpling Street, desperately hoping to reach Scallywags School before the town hall clock struck two…

Chapter Twelve

*Bong...Bong...*rang the bell in the distance as Sherwood and Patty finally turned down School Lane to make their way to the teachers' car park at the back of Scallywags School.

Even though Sherwood had his siren blaring and blue light flashing, his motorcycle and Patty's van had been held up on more than one occasion on their way there...

The first problem they came across was as soon as they turned out of Dumpling Street to head down to the seafront. There they met Sue Magoo, driving her Fiat 500 the wrong way up the one-way system.

"You're on a one-way street, Miss Magoo," Sherwood shouted.

"I know, young lady!" Sue Magoo replied, "That's why I'm only going the one way, isn't it?"

"But it's totally the wrong way, Sue," shouted Patty through her car window, "didn't you see any of the road signs?"

"What road signs?" Sue Magoo said, peering all around her.

"Put your glasses on and you'll see them," Patty replied, tapping her steering wheel in frustration.

"I would if I could find the blessed things, dear," Sue Magoo tutted, bashing the horn of her car, "now will you please move your motorcycle, miss, and turn that awfully loud racket you're playing off, it's giving me quite a headache…"

It took Sherwood a couple of minutes to convince Sue Magoo that she needed to reverse and another minute for him to drive her Fiat 500 when she told him that she couldn't actually see out of the back window of her car…

Finally, they were on their way again. But no sooner had they begun to get up a head of steam in their vehicles than obstacle number two stopped them dead in their tracks as the sped through the colourful carnival parade which was slowly making its way along the seafront.

Many of the floats immediately pulled to one side of the road on hearing the police siren, allowing Sherwood and Patty to pass them by. All was going well until one float, an exact replica of the longboat that Scally the Wag had landed on the shores of the bay in, decided to '*invade*' Patty's van to '*steal*' all of her wares...

However, the four teenage Vikings soon stopped trying to hijack it, fleeing in terror at the sight of the huge Maine Coon cat who jumped out of the sidecar and began to chase them along the seafront.

Watson growled angrily at them, as all bar one of the teenagers ran across the beach and dived into the sea for safety whilst their lone, stray friend cowered behind one of the posts under the old town pier until Watson finally sloped away.

"Normally I'd have told you off for scaring people like that, old friend," Sherwood said as they finally got under way again, turning the motorcycle to go up the lane that was just before the land slip, "but not today, my dear Watson…"

By now, Sherwood knew that they would have to get a move on to reach the school in time up his accelerator, Patty's van racing to catch up with him from behind.

All was going well until they reached the road which would eventually lead them to the turning for School Lane.

"I don't believe this," Sherwood said, slowing his motorcycle down as a herd of sheep slowly made their way along the road in front of them, their owner Rusty Gates trudging behind them, his shepherd's crook in hand.

"Can you hurry up please, Rusty," Sherwood shouted, standing up on his footboards, "this is an emergency."

"I'm going as fast as I possibly can, constable," the tall shepherd grumbled, "but as you can see, Colin the collie's not with me today to help round them up, so there's no way I can gee them up to move along any faster than they already are..."

"Mew, mew, mew-mew, mew, mew-mew," Watson pleaded, already poised to leap from sidecar for a second time that afternoon."

"Only if you promise not to bite any of them," Sherwood smiled as Watson leapt out and began to stalk the sheep, doing his very best sheep*cat* impersonation...

It wasn't long before the sheep reached the field where they normally grazed, Watson gently herding the last one in before running back to jump into the sidecar again as Rusty Gates waved them on their way.

"Going to be lucky to even make two o'clock now," Sherwood muttered to himself as he increased his speed, Patty doing the same behind him.

So it was that the five of them eventually parked up in the teachers' car park just as the town hall's chimes slowly began to ebb away in the distance.

Charlie and Holly stood opened mouthed as they looked out across the school field, it now being full of people who were visiting the dozens of stalls and food stands which stretched out as far as the eye could see.

"Come on, you two," Sherwood said as he began to load the cheesecake boxes into both of their arms, "there will be plenty of time for all that later." Charlie and Holly nodded as they rushed after Patty and Sherwood with their cheesecake towers stacked high, Watson staying behind to protect the boxes which were still in the back of Patty's van, waiting to be unloaded.

"In here," Patty said, ducking through the entrance of a huge tent which had a sign saying '*The Scallywag Bay Bake Off*' pinned to the side of the canvas.

Charlie and Holly were both delighted to see their teacher, Miss Wright standing talking to someone at the far end of the tent. However, their smiles were soon wiped off their faces once they realised that the person she was talking to was wearing a white baker's hat and coat just like the one Patty was wearing that day.

"We're already too late," Patty sighed as she saw that the tables Miss Wright and the other baker were stood beside were full of a variety of delicious looking cakes.

"Patty, we didn't think you were going to make it in time," a voice suddenly said from behind them.

Sherwood, Patty and the twins all turned to see the friendly figure of Mr Read, the deputy headteacher, smiling at them in disbelief.

"Obviously," Patty said sulkily, "looks like you couldn't wait to place the order with that other baker either, doesn't it?"

"It's not like that, Patty," Mr Read smiled, "Robin – that's the name of the baker from Hogswash - turned up earlier on the off-chance that you'd not get here in time, that's all."

"Still means it's all been a waste of time making these cheesecakes though," Patty sighed.

"On the contrary, we've more than enough room for them now!" a woman's voice suddenly said.

Sherwood and the others turned to look into Miss Wright's bright and sunny face, Robin the Hogswash Baker standing beside her, now looking slightly disappointed.

"It just so happens that we had a call from Farmer Plowright earlier," Miss Wright continued, "she was supposed to have a cheese stand here today but sadly can't make it now…"

"Something about having some technical issues with her quad bike or something," Mr Read added, "so you'll be doing us a favour by being a last-minute substitute for her."

"As the stall is already paid for, any money you make from selling your cheesecakes will be yours to keep," Miss Wright said, "which is likely to be a lot more than you would have got from the school had you supplied us the cakes for the party."

"So, what do you say?" Mr Read asked hopefully.

"Hmmm, let me see..." Patty said, pretending to think for a minute, "the answer's yes of course!"

Everyone cheered in delight, all except Robin the Hogswash Baker that is, who now looked even more crest-fallen than he did before.

"Cheer up, young man," Sherwood said, "you'll still get the money you must have so desperately wanted to earn today by already being here before we arrived."

"What makes you think I was only after the money?" the young man snapped, "I was merely offering to help out of the kindness of my heart."

"And as we said, we can't thank you enough for doing so, Robin," Mr Read replied.

"Well, as everything seems to have worked out for the best, I'll be on my way then," Robin said, turning to leave.

"But we haven't paid you for your cakes yet," Miss

Wright said, "wait until the party's over and we'll sort the cash out for you."

"Don't worry about it, I've all the money I need, honestly, I'm just happy to have helped," Robin said nervously, beginning to shuffle away from the teacher."

"But how? It must have cost you a fortune to make all of these wonderful cakes," Mr Read added, "at least let us cover your baking costs."

Robin slowly continued to inch towards the exit to the tent, shaking his head as he did so.

"No need, really. By the time I'd finished baking this morning, I realised that I had far more cakes than I actually needed," Robin stuttered, "So, before I came here, I went around all of the other villages such as Codswallop, Piffle, Bunkum and Balderdash. I sold them my leftover cakes for their own street parties and summer fetes. That made me more than enough to cover my costs and expenses. I'm happy for you to have these cakes on me."

"Are you sure, Robin?" Miss Wright smiled, "It's awfully kind of you."

"Think nothing of it - consider them a gift," Robin said as he quickly began to scurry away, only to then stop dead in his tracks at the sight of the huge cat who now blocked the exit to the tent.

"Don't be so hasty, Robin, come stay with us and enjoy today's celebrations with us," Sherwood said, walking up to the young man before wrapping a strong arm around the baker's shoulders.

Robin twitched and shook his head repeatedly, his white hat flopping back and forth as he did so.

"Er, no, it's…it's all right, thanks," he stuttered, sweat now beginning to coat his brow, "like I said, I'm just glad everything has worked out for the best after your troubles this weekend, Patty."

"Thank you, Robin," Patty smiled.

"Yes, seeing you and your friends happy is more than payment enough," Robin replied, his face starting to flush slightly, "now I'll be on my way."

"Nonsense," Sherwood said, now fully sensing that there was something suspicious but also strangely familiar about the young baker, "there's no need to blush - you deserve everything you've got coming to you, young man…"

"You're much too kind," Robin stuttered, trying to pull away from Sherwood's tight embrace, "but now I really must be on my way."

"No stay…I insist," Sherwood replied, noticing how red in the face Robin had become as the baker tried to pull his hat further down over his brow.

"There's no need for you to be embarrassed, Robin," Patty smiled, "what you did today was really thoughtful and considerate."

"So why don't you take off that big old hat of yours off and come join the party!" Sherwood laughed, "Let your hair down for a few hours or so!"

"No, no, it's quite all right, really," Robin replied, his face now getting redder and redder by the second.

"No...I insist," said Sherwood loudly, whipping off the baker's hat - only to find that Robin's bushy mop of red hair was still attached to it!

"Oh dear, I'm terribly sorry," Sherwood said, "but it really does appear that you've let your hair down quite literally!"

"No, it's all right," the baker growled, his now blonde fringe stuck to his forehead as he desperately tried to put his hat and wig back on again.

"Wait a minute..." Patty gasped, pointing at the baker's face, "you also appear to be losing all of your beard too!

Sherwood peered at the curly red beard which had slowly begun to slide off Robin's sweaty chin.

"Let me help you with that," Sherwood said, reaching both his arms forward.

"Honestly, it's no bother..." the baker stuttered as he tried to wriggle away from Sherwood's grasp.

But as he did so, his beard came away in the police constable's hands, leaving the baker's face clean and smooth shaven for all to clearly see.

Everybody gasped as they suddenly realised that the friendly baker was not actually a man at all and that they were now looking at a young woman instead.

"Sue Cheff!" Patty exclaimed, staring directly into the face of her summer helper.

"Just as I suspected," said Sherwood, placing a hand on Sue's shoulder, "it was you who broke into Patty's bakery and stole both her ingredients and her cakes, wasn't it?"

Sue bowed her head, sighed and nodded, her long straw-blonde hair now covering her eyes.

"Yes, PC Holmes," she said quietly, "I thought it would be a good way to make some extra money before I go back to university. I'm ever so sorry, Patty. I promise that I'll never do anything like this ever again, pinky-swear."

"It's ok, Sue, we know how tough it is being a student. After all, we once were poor students too ourselves, were we not Sherwood? Patty smiled, looking at the police constable, "we both forgive you, don't we?"

"No, we do not, Patty," Sherwood surprisingly said, "you see, I wondered why you looked slightly familiar to me the first time we met and - like Sue Magoo - I never forget a face…"

Everyone watched in amazement as Sherwood grabbed the back of Sue's hair and ripped it off…to reveal a full head of short, black hair hidden beneath it instead.

"Ladies and gentlemen," Sherwood said, holding the blonde wig high in the air, "may I present to you Miss Molly Hardy, the great-great-great-granddaughter of Sherlock Holmes' arch-enemy and greatest foe, Professor James Moriarty…"

Chapter Thirteen

Patty and the others gasped as a cheeky smile filled Molly Hardy's face as she turned and winked at Sherwood.

"Hello again Sherwood, missed me?" she smiled, "Took you long enough to work out it was me, though, didn't it?"

"Only because I thought you were still in London," Sherwood frowned, "what made you come all the way to Scallywag Bay?"

"Like I said, I missed you, Sherwood-baby," Molly Hardy grinned as she wiped the glue which had held her beard in place off her face, "things weren't the same after you left."

"You mean it was harder for you to rob people there, more like," Sherwood sighed, "especially as there are now better police officers than me keeping a close eye on you."

"Oh, you're a much better detective than you think,

Sherwood," Molly Hardy grinned, "after all, you did catch me – eventually!"

"What are we going to do with her now?" Patty asked as a crowd began to gather in the tent, waiting for Mr Learner to arrive.

"Don't you worry about Molly," Sherwood replied, snapping a handcuff onto Molly Hardy's wrist before attaching it to his, "she won't be going anywhere for a while."

"Let's go and get the rest of the cheesecakes from the van," Charlie said as a crowd began to gather around Patty's stall,

"Yes, but hurry," Holly shouted, "they're buying them as fast as we're cutting them!"

Once the van had been emptied, Sherwood and Molly sat at the cake stand, watching Patty's cheesecake stall sell out minutes before Mr Learner arrived for his surprise farewell party.

Sherwood unlocked the handcuffs and looked at

Molly sternly.

"Time for you to start making amends, young lady," he growled.

"I was afraid you were going to say that," Molly Hardy frowned as everyone gathered around Mr Learner and began queuing for a slice of one his retirement cakes.

"First, I want you to smile as you serve cake to all my wonderful Scallywag Bay friends who have helped us this weekend," Sherwood whispered before continuing, "then after the party is over, you can do all the clearing up as well as all the washing and tidying up for all the stalls here today."

"Anything else you want me to do whilst I'm at it?" Molly Hardy sarcastically asked through gritted teeth as she began to dish out cake slices to all the townspeople.

"There is actually," Sherwood said, adding, "I want you to use the money you got from all the other villages to pay for the damage that you've caused to

Patty's bakery, as well as all the ingredients you stole from her Friday night."

Molly looked sheepishly at the police constable as he continued.

"Also, as you'll get at least six months' community service for your crimes this weekend," Sherwood added, "I want you spend that time working for free in Patty's bakery as a way of apologising to her. Understand?"

"Yes, Sherwood," sighed Molly Hardy, "she must be a very special friend of yours that baker."

"All my friends here in Scallywag Bay are special in their own way, Molly," Sherwood said as Patty, Charlie and Holly made their way to the stall, "that's why your dastardly deeds completely failed in the end. People around here look after one another, especially in times of need."

Patty smiled as another crowd of people, disappointed to see that the cheesecake stall had already sold out, surged towards Molly Hardy's cake stand instead. Molly looked desperately at Sherwood, her eyes pleading for help.

"Well, don't just stand there," the police constable said, shrugging his shoulders, "it looks like you've well over a hundred hungry customers who want to have their cake and eat it, so you'd better get serving!"

Sherwood sat at the back of stall for the rest of Mr Learner's party, smiling as he watched Molly struggle to keep up with the cries and demands of her hungry customers, the young woman now being totally rushed off her feet.

"Serves Miss Hardy right for being so naughty!" Sherwood whispered to himself as Charlie and Holly handed him a large piece of Black Forest cake.

"This looks absolutely amazing, Patty!" Sherwood gasped, grabbing a plastic fork.

"Doesn't it?" Patty replied, adding, "I only wish it had been me who'd made it…"

Sherwood looked up, first at Patty and then at Molly Hardy before shaking his head in disbelief.

"Well, I never..." he said as he broke a piece of the cake off and lifted it to his lips.

Patty and the twins watched eagerly, Watson drooling at his feet as Sherwood slowly chewed the cake, licking his lips and closing his eyes as he swallowed his first mouthful.

"Well...?" Patty asked eagerly.

Sherwood looked down at the plate before raising his head to smile a chocolaty smile at her.

"Do you know what, Patty," said Sherwood as he took another bite of it, "I have to admit that Molly's a much better master baker than she is a master criminal...have a taste of this, will you?"

Sherwood grabbed another plastic fork and cut a bit of the chocolate cake before offering it to Patty who gratefully ate it.

"Oh my god," the baker gasped in amazement, "that's so incredibly light and moist, it just melts on your tongue! You're right – she's an excellent baker, I'd go as far as saying that she's even better than I was at her age."

"Perhaps you can help her to see that a life of crime doesn't pay but a life of cake does!" Sherwood smiled as he wolfed down the rest of his cake.

"I'll do my best," Patty replied, "but it takes a long time and a lot of dedication to become a master baker."

"Well, Molly will have plenty of time to practice when she does her community service with you, won't she?" Sherwood smiled.

"That she will," said Patty before adding, "once again, thank you all for your help this weekend."

"It was our pleasure," Holly replied, her brother happily nodding beside her.

"Anytime you need our help, we'll be there in future, PC Holmes," Charlie eagerly added.

"I'll be sure to remember that kids," Sherwood smiled, "you were a great help to me - even if the

Merry Widows gave you both the creeps!"

"And thank you, Sherwood, for finally solving such a tricky mystery," Patty said, kissing Sherwood gently on the cheek.

"Please, think nothing of it," Sherwood blushed, Watson and the twins winking and nudging one another as he continued, "in the end it was all quite *cake-a-mentary,* my dear Patty!"

Sherwood Holmes and Watson the Cat will return...

Also by Jonas Lane

Slipp In Time
Grammarticus
The Last of the Unicorns
Slipp, Sliding Away
Poppy Copperthwaite:
Spellcaster
Locked Down
Another Time, Slipp!
Dragon Chasers:
The Knight School
Nona's Ark
Suped and Duped
There's Many a Slipp!
Wilde and Dangerous Things
Poetic Licence
Poppy Copperthwaite:
Spelldemic
Sherwood Holmes:
The Great Cake Robbery

All book titles available to purchase from
www.JonasLaneAuthor.com
or by ordering from amazon.co.uk

Slipp In Time

After two young cousins are left home alone to their own mischievous devices one lazy afternoon, little do they know the harm their actions will eventually have on the course of history...

Whilst out delivering newspapers, Alex and Georgie McClellan meet and befriend the eccentric inventor Lord Thyme-Slipp who claims to have designed his own homemade time machine, much to their initial surprise and disbelief...

However, later that day, after using Georgie's father's computer against his express wishes, the children are forced to turn to Slipp for help in the hope he can take them just a few hours back in time to undo the damage they've done, with no one being any the wiser...

But a nervous cat and a violent storm propel the three of them hundreds of years, back into the past, to a time when the world caught fire, where their innocent actions there change both the *then* and the *now* to even more disastrous effect...

Grammarticus

Mind your language...watch what you say...the pen is mightier than the sword and way more deadly!

When a small group of school friends, faced with the prospect of failing their impending SATs tests, stumble across an old and mysterious grammar book, they think that their prayers have finally been answered.

Instead, Grammarticus poses them more questions than answers, setting them on a deadly collision course with an evil teacher intent on using the book and its secrets for herself...

The Last of the Unicorns

When Alun and Ceri Licht were evacuated to their grandparents in Wales at the start of the Second World War, they expected to find the love which they lacked from their parents in London…

What they didn't expect to find was something that would change their lives forever…

A mythical creature hidden away from the world…

A centuries-old evil waiting to rise from the darkness…

Friendships which would last an eternity…

And an adventure unlike no other…

Slipp Sliding Away!

Slipp, Alex and Georgie are back - literally!

Our misadventurers are finally home but discover it to be a totally different world to the one they left less than twenty-four hours before…

Returning to school after their holidays, the children are shocked to discover all they once knew is no more, replaced by an alternative history where an infamous name from the past now dominates the present…

Realising that they may be responsible for this strange, new world, Alex and Georgie have no choice but to again ask for help from their friend, the eccentric inventor Lord Thyme-Slipp, to right the wrongs caused by their actions. Using his not-so-technical no-how, Slipp has modified the Time Skipper to return them to the exact point in the past where fate intervened to change the future…

But a careless mistake and an uncanny coincidence scupper their plans as they find themselves plunged into the middle of a deadly argument between two powerful and ambitious men who hold the fate of a kingdom in their hands…

Poppy Copperthwaite
Spellcaster

Born into a community of Majeeks, on her 18th birthday - her *Coming of Mage* – Poppy Copperthwaite finally expected to discover the magical powers buried deep within her in order to claim her birthright and eventually rule her parents' kingdom. Instead, her hopes and dreams are left in tatters when the cruel, fickle finger of fate conspires against her, leaving Poppy desperately hoping to find a way to unlock and unleash her true Majeek potential.

Sent to a magical and mystical foundation, Poppy faces a frantic race against time, whilst taking part in a series of tests and experiments to discover what type of spellcaster she is, under the watchful eye of the spellcialist, Doctor Leopold Harryhausen.

But with the clock ticking and her enemies plotting and conspiring against her, can Poppy and her group of weird and dysfunctional friends - a rude and grumpy boggart, a legendary witch and another teenage Majeek, lost somewhere between time - find a way to let loose the dormant powers trapped within her so that Poppy Copperthwaite can truly become the spellcaster she was always destined to be...?

Locked Down

From the pen of Jonas Lane comes a collection of tales, both old and new, which are sure to amuse and confuse, as well as sending tiny shivers of fear tingling down his readers' spines.

Gathered together for the very first time, *Locked Down,* his collection of tall, dark and twisted tales includes sixteen short stories, novelettes and teaser texts which cross a range of different genres and writing styles.

For those of you new to his writing, Jonas Lane's *Locked Down* will leave you wanting to read even more...

Another Time, Slipp!

Slipp is back - way back!
Having escaped the bloody battle of Hastings in the nick of time, Slipp, Alex and Georgie find that they are - yet again - far from home, lost somewhere in the past.
With the Time Skipper badly damaged our misadventures find themselves stranded in an England still recovering from an attack by one of its deadliest rivals, where the locals are suspicious of strangers and their intentions.

Predictably, it's not too long before Slipp, Alex and Georgie find themselves pitched into a bitter war of words between two of history's finest and most famous heroes and adventurers…

Faced with finding a way to somehow escape the past in order to somehow correct the future, our terrible trio yet again bumble their way through a bygone world where words speak louder than actions...

Dragon Chasers:
The Knight School

A group of gifted youngsters presented with the chance of a lifetime when offered the opportunity of a free scholarship at one of England's finest, but most elusive, schools.

An ancient evil hiding amongst us, having watched, and plotted our demise for thousands of years, waiting for the moment to strike again.

A secret society tasked with defending humankind, protecting us from a legendary enemy who seeks to return from the shadows and reclaim a world they believe to be rightfully theirs once more.

Part Harry Potter, part Da Vinci Code, all action and adventure, *The Knight School* is the first, gripping adventure in the Dragonchasers series.

Here be dragons...

Nona's Ark

Twelve-year-old Nona Lancaster thought her life was finally on the up, having moved to the school of her dreams spending each and every day playing sports with her best friends.

However, a sudden, final unexpected and unwanted gift from her secret grandfather soon turned her life on its head.

Faced with a desperate race against time to thwart her new brother's evil plans for the zoo she too now owned, Nona and her friends embark on the adventure of a lifetime to rescue the animals her grandfather had devoted his life to...

A madcap story in the style of the classic 1950s Ealing Comedies, *Nona's Ark* is an adventure for all ages!

Suped and Duped

Have you ever been caught up in an argument with other people? You know, when there's just three of you and two of them totally disagree about something or other...

Or there's been an inexplicable falling out between them and you're trapped in the middle of it, desperately trying hard not to pick sides...

It's a difficult enough position for any teenager to normally be in but imagine what it would be like if you were forced into it by very extraordinary circumstances...*super* circumstances in fact...

That's the awkward situation three lifelong school friends - AJ Sipowicz, Kai Kennedy and Mez Monroe – suddenly find themselves in when two of them develop strange and mysterious superpowers whilst begging the third member of their friendship group to keep their secrets safe, especially from one another...

But when moral intentions and personal motives clash, putting AJ, Kai and Mez on a direct collision course with those in authority regarding the fate of their city, they are forced to choose between right and wrong, good and evil, to save their friendships and to protect their families' futures forever...

There's Many a Slipp!

Time just got a whole lot more confusing and complicated for Slipp, Alex and Georgie...

Arriving in 1966, our three misadventurers soon discover an England much different to the one Slipp remembered growing up in - ruled by those far less tolerant of others...

Accused of stealing one of the world's most famous and iconic items, Slipp, Alex and Georgie are immediately pitched into an adventure where fate, family and freedom conflict with one another as they try to find a way to reset history once more...

Wilde and Dangerous Things

Little did reporter Mason Adams know when answering the newspaper advertisement about working for a detective living in Baker Street how his life would suddenly and dramatically change forever. However, rather than being employed by the world-famous person he was expecting to meet, Mason instead finds himself working with Cordelia Wilde, a brilliant cryptobiologist, haunted by her past, who hunts monsters for a living…

Soon, Wilde and Mason are joined on their adventures by Julliette, a young French girl escaping her family, hoping to take control of her future. Before long, they find themselves on the trail of a legendary murderer, their hunt taking them from the dark and deadly streets of the East End of London to the mysterious wilds of Dartmoor…

Secretly watched by those seeking to stop the truth from ever being revealed to the world, will the three young and irregular detectives eventually discover the secrets of the wicked and dangerous things that lurk in the shadows of Victorian England…?

Poppy Copperthwaite
Spelldemic

When Magda, a young Majeek orphan and refugee, arrives at the Foundation having escaped from a secret medical facility in her homeland, little do Poppy Copperthwaite, her family and friends know of the mysterious and dangerous threat she carries inside her and the life-changing effect it will have on those she accidentally encounters…

Just weeks after first meeting one another, Poppy and Magda find themselves relentlessly hunted by an evil alliance of NORMs and Majeeks - led by a devious and ruthless Prime Minister - who want Magda's magical secrets to increase their powers and abilities in order to realise their ambitions of ruling over all others…

Can Poppy, Humphry the boggart, Gil and Doctor Harryhausen hide and protect the young girl they've quickly grown to care for, keeping her safe from capture, whilst they embark on a desperate race against time to try to save the lives of those they love…

Sherwood Holmes:
The Great Cake Robbery

A detective by the name of Holmes...
His loyal and faithful friend, Watson...
And a strange mystery to solve...

Except this isn't the world-famous Sherlock Holmes of 221B Baker Street - it's his great-great-great-great nephew, Constable Sherwood Holmes of the Scallywag Bay Police instead...

Having recently moved to the sleepy seaside town, keen to escape the hustle and bustle of the crime-filled streets of London, the last thing Sherwood expected to do was solve a robbery at the local bakery, not once, but twice, on the most important and celebrated weekend in Scallywag Bay's yearly calendar.

Helped by his oldest friend, a huge Maine Coon cat called Watson, and the young twins, Charlie and Holly Jones, can Sherwood help his friend, Patty Cake, meet the most important delivery date of her life, or will they all be left with just a few crumbs of comfort, having been foiled by a sticky-fingered thief who always seems to be one step ahead of them...

Praise from the readers of Jonas Lane's books

"As an avid reader, I know when I've found something special when I can't pull myself away from a book. I read Slipp In Time in only a few hours and loved every minute of it! I laughed, giggled, had to pause due to said giggling, and then I laughed some more. It's a brilliant story, and I highly recommend it for children and adults alike."

"Loved it! Great to read a kids' book that has pace adventure and humour. Having the main protagonists as a boy and a girl means that any child can identify with the story. What's not to like about time travel on a sofa! Watch out for 'Hamster Ragu' and 'pomegranate shootout'! As an English teacher, this is one I will definitely be reading with my students. Looking forward to the next one.... did I mention the tantalising cliffhanger at the end?"

"A really good adventure of two young children on a journey, including history and good humour. Kids will definitely enjoy this book and with a cliffhanger like that will be eagerly awaiting the next episode and adventure!"

"I bought this book for my 10-year-old daughter. Despite being an avid reader, she always chooses very similar reading styles (cute puppies, girls having sleepovers, blah blah!) Therefore, I wanted to help widen her reading world. Boy did this book fit the brief! Engaging characters and a writing style that made her want a second book immediately! Can't wait for the sequel!!"

"Excellent read from start to finish. Could not stop turning the pages once I started."

"… brilliant for children and teenagers that love an adventure."

"Fantastic book! Bought this for my 11-year-old son to encourage him to read… he loved it and can't wait for more!"

"I bought this for my 9-year-old daughter who loves anything to do with science and time travel! She absolutely loved it and read it in a couple of days. Well written and easy to comprehend and fitting with today's society. Bring on the next one!"

"Bought this book for myself…loved the imagination of the author…would recommend it to anyone who loves to read and put themselves into the story. Look forward to his and my next journey!"

"Fantastic…loved the story and the references to history. Can't wait for the next book to see what's happened. What a cliffhanger!"

"A fantastic read, suited for all ages, with relatable characters and an interesting plot. The book has a brilliant ending that has left me wanting the second instalment already!"

"Amazing and clever storyline that kept my 8-year-old daughter (and us!) hooked!! What a cliffhanger at the end! Cannot wait to read the next one and really hope there will be more. Excellent!!!"

"A very good read for children and adults. Includes time travel, humour and history. I will recommend this book and I think it'll encourage more children to read!"

"Great follow up, well worth the wait, my son loved it!"

"Bought this book for my seven-year-old son. He really enjoyed it, as did I! Believable characters, funny situations with good links to real events in history. We are both looking forward to the next Slipp story!"

"A lovely story, cleverly written. Once you start to read it you can't put it down. Great characters and plot make it seem perfect for a typical British film."

"Brilliant...This should be rated six stars!"

"Really enjoyed this, suitable for all ages, needs to be a film!"

"...most writers write in a similar way, but Jonas Lane doesn't...that's what makes his books unlike any others."

"My children are reluctant readers and this book has engaged both my children aged 9 and 13 to read, my youngest said this book is fun and exciting. My 13-year-old is dyslexic and has read very few books from cover to cover but he read all this one, so thank you for this book being accessible for all, looking forward to the next one."

"A fantastic read, suited for all ages, with relatable characters and an interesting plot. The book has a brilliant ending that has left me wanting the second instalment already!

"Captivating...Just finished reading this novel with my 6-year-old. We loved it and it had her gripped throughout. Loved how the ending left us wanting more. Fortunately, we have the second novel to hand ready to start straight away!

"A very good read for children and adults. Includes time travel, humour and history. I will recommend this book and I think it'll encourage more children to read."

"My teaching assistant bought the Slipp books and read them to my class during lunch. When we started a new genre – adventure stories – in English, my children were so inspired that they created their own time travel stories! These books really helped my class to develop their own characters and problems that they had to resolve. I would recommend this book to all teachers as I was able to help develop and then read stories that my class were very proud of writing."

"Fantastic story about 2 children on an adventure. Loved the story and the references to history. Can't wait for the next book to see what's happened. What a cliffhanger!"

"Fantastic easy read story for all ages, adventure and history all in one. Ends with a great cliffhanger can't wait for the next adventure."

"After reading the first book in this series, both

my eldest daughter and I were desperate to get our hands on this next book! Once again Jonas Lane hasn't disappointed with his well-balanced mix of humour and history. The easy to read style of these brilliant books means that my youngest daughter now is wanting to join in. Hopefully, the next one is in the pipeline, so we can all have one each!!!!"

"Super sequel! Great book - my daughter loved it"

"A heartwarming story full of humour, excitement and morality. Written in a dynamic rhythm that keeps you willfully entranced!"

"Five Stars!"

Thanks to all those that have left such wonderful comments. Authors and writers live or die by the reviews given by their readers. Please take a moment to share your opinions and leave a review by visiting the site that you purchased this book from.

Alternatively, visit Jonas at his website as he would welcome your feedback.

www.jonaslaneauthor.com

Printed in Great Britain
by Amazon